# Security Concerns & Strategic Policy of Southeast Asia & the Pacific

# Security Concerns and Strategic Policy of Southeast Asia and the Pacific

**Hargovind Joshi**

**FORWARD BOOKS**
NEW DELHI • GUWAHATI • VISAKHAPATNAM

**FORWARD BOOKS**
4649-B/21, Ansari Road
Darya Ganj, New Delhi - 110 002
Ph.: 23263193 / 9811582579 / 09435116718
Fax: 011-23263193
Email: ektabooks@yahoo.com
www.akanshapublishinghouse.com

*Security Concerns and Strategic Policy of Southeast Asia and the Pacific*



First Published 2011

ISBN 978-81-909742-3-3



PRINTED IN INDIA

Published by Forward Books, New Delhi and Printed at S.N. Printers, Delhi.

# Contents

# Preface

It is significant to note that in defence and military atlas of the world, Southeast Asia and the Pacific region is hotbed of activities and security concerns. Its strategeic location is the concern of USA and Western Europe more particularly besides China and Japan.

Geographically along the western rim of the Pacific there is no equivalent of the regional fault that has divided east and west in Europe since 1945. The security equation is dominated by two very different factors. The first, and most potent, factor is the intersection, in the northern part of the region, of great-Power interests and strategic concerns on the part of the four most powerful countries in the world—China, Japan, the Russia and the United States of America. The second factor is the perpetuation, in different parts of the region, of ancient enmities, linked sometimes with religious or ideological fervour, or exacerbated by differences between rich and poor and—often enough—by the intervention of outside powers.

The mosaic of Asian-Pacific nations is made up of many nationalities and cultures; the geography is disparate and difficult; most significant of all, in terms of the security preoccupations of the region, power is unevenly spread. The single most striking feature is diversity.

In the present book all pertinent issues of security concerns and strategic policies of Southeast Asia and the Pacific region are addressed elaborately in analytic way. Though in present times unipolar world security equations change frequently, yet we have tried to portray the picture in the historical context as well as the present day scenario.

The vital information is collated under the following chapters—An Introduction of Southeast Asia; Asian-Pacific Region: Changing Scenario; South-East Asian Security Issues and Confidence-building; Arms Limitations in the Asia-Pacific Region: Issues and Prospect; The Korean Peninsula: Security Concerns and CBMs; Arms Control in the Korean Peninsula; ASEAN on Security Concerns in South-East Asia and the Pacific; ASEAN Countries on Openness and Transparency; Towards A New Regional Order; Koreas on Regional Security; Malaysian Army: A Study; Appendices and Bibliography etc.

Definitely, this will serve as a reference book for academics, defence and strategic analysts, policy planners and administrators besides general readers concerned with cause of peace and security.

In fact, we have drawn upon works of many experts in the field while collating the information. We express our gratefulness to them all. Though every care is taken to furnish accurate information, there may have crept in some inaccuracies, which we will rectify if brought to our notice by learned readers. Simultaneously, are also grateful to our colleagues and friends for inspiring, guiding and assisting us in different stages of this work. Finally I am thankful to my publishers for evincing interest in this and publishing it meticulously in superb manner.

**—HGJ**

# 1

# An Introduction of Southeast Asia

Since we are concerned here to delineate security and strategic matters of Southeast Asia, first we must have a thorough understanding of the history, geography, society and politics of the region.

**Basic Facts**

| *Country* | *Area (km2)* | *Population (2009)* | *Density (/km2)* | *GDP USD (2009)* | *GDP per capita (2009)* | *Capital* |
|---|---|---|---|---|---|---|
| Brunei | 5,765 | 400,000 | 70 | 14,700,000,000 | $36,700 | Bandar Seri Begawan |
| Myanmar | 676,578 | 50,020,000 | 74 | 26,820,000,000 | $500 | Naypyidaw |
| Cambodia | 181,035 | 14,805,000 | 82 | 10,900,000,000 | $800 | Phnom Penh |
| Timor-Leste | 14,874 | 1,134,000 | 76 | 599,000,000 | $500 | Dili |
| Indonesia | 1,904,569 | 240,271,522 | 126 | 514,900,000,000 | $2,200 | Jakarta |
| Laos | 236,800 | 6,320,000 | 27 | 5,721,000,000 | $900 | Vientiane |
| Malaysia | 329,847 | 28,318,000 | 83 | 191,400,000,000 | $6,800 | Kuala Lumpur |
| Philippines | 299,764 | 91,983,000 | 307 | 158,700,000,000 | $1,750 | Manila |
| Singapore | 710.2 | 4,987,600 | 7,023 | 177,100,000,000 | $35,500 | City of Singapore (Downtown Core) |
| Thailand | 513,120 | 67,764,000 | 132 | 263,500,000,000 | $3,900 | Bangkok |
| Vietnam | 331,210 | 88,069,000 | 265 | 97,120,000,000 | $1,100 | Hanoi |

**Territories**

| *Territory* | *Area (km²)* | *Population* | *Density (/km²)* |
|---|---|---|---|
| Christmas Island | 135 | 1,402 | 10.4 |
| Cocos (Keeling) Islands | 14 | 596 | 42.6 |

Southeast Asia is a subregion of Asia, consisting of the

countries that are geographically south of China, east of India and north of Australia. The region lies on the intersection of geological plates, with heavy seismic and volcanic activity.

Southeast Asia consists of two geographic regions: the Asian mainland and island arcs and archipelagoes to the east and southeast. The mainland section consists of Burma, Cambodia, Laos, Thailand, Vietnam and Peninsular Malaysia while the maritime section consists of Brunei, East Malaysia, East Timor, Indonesia, the Philippines, and Singapore. Papua New Guinea is an observer in the Association of Southeast Asian Nations, as is East Timor.

Geographically speaking southern China, Taiwan, Hong Kong and Macau are sometimes grouped in the Southeast Asia subregion, although politically they are rarely grouped as such. The same is true for the Andaman and Nicobar Islands of India.

Austronesian peoples predominate in this region. The major religions are Islam and Buddhism, followed by Christianity. However, a wide variety of religions are found throughout the region, including many Hindu and animist-influenced practices.

**Countries of the Region**

- Brunei
- Cambodia
- East Timor (Timor-Leste)
- Indonesia
- Laos
- Malaysia
- Myanmar
- Philippines
- Singapore
- Thailand
- Vietnam

Excluding Timor-Leste all other countries are members of the Association of Southeast Asian Nations (ASEAN). The area, together with part of South Asia, was widely known as the East Indies or simply the Indies until the 20th century. Christmas Island and the Cocos (Keeling) Islands are considered part of Southeast Asia though they are governed by Australia. Sovereignty issues exist over some islands in the South China Sea. Papua is politically part of Southeast Asia through Indonesia, although geographically it is often considered as part of Oceania. As of 2009, Papua New Guinea has stated that it might join ASEAN, indicating a possible switch in its geographic locale.

Geogeographically, the eastern parts of Indonesia and East Timor (east of Wallace Line) are considered to be geographically parts of Oceania.

Southeast Asia is geographically divided into two subregions, namely Mainland Southeast Asia (or Indochina) and Maritime Southeast Asia (or the similarly defined Malay Archipelago).

**Mainland Southeast Asia**

- Cambodia
- Laos
- Myanmar (Burma)
- Thailand
- Vietnam
- Peninsular Malaysia

**Maritime Southeast Asia**

- East Malaysia
- Brunei
- Indonesia
- Philippines

- Singapore
- Timor-Leste

It is remarkable that the Andaman and Nicobar Islands of India are geographically considered part of Southeast Asia. Bangladesh and the Seven Sister States of India are culturally part of Southeast Asia and sometimes considered both South Asian and Southeast Asian. The Seven Sister States of India are also geographically part of southeast Asia. Hainan Island and several other southern Chinese regions such as Yunnan, Guizhou and Guangxi are considered both East Asian and Southeast Asian. The rest of New Guinea is sometimes included so are Palau, Guam, and the Northern Mariana Islands, which were all part of the Spanish East Indies.

The region has been inhabited by men by around 45,000 years ago. Austronesian people, who form the majority of the modern population in Indonesia and the Philippines, migrated to South East Asia from Taiwan. They arrived in Indonesia around 2000 BCE, and as they spread through the archipelago, confined the native Melanesian peoples to the far eastern regions.

Solheim and others have shown evidence for a *Nusantao* (*Nusantara*) maritime trading network ranging from Vietnam to the rest of the archipelago as early as 5000 BCE to 1 CE. The peoples of Southeast Asia, especially those of Austronesian descent, have been seafarers for thousands of years, some reaching the island of Madagascar. Their vessels, such as the vinta, were ocean-worthy. Magellan's voyage records how much more maneuvreable their vessels were, as compared to the European ships.

Passage through the Indian Ocean aided the colonization of Madagascar by the Austronesian people, as well as commerce between West Asia and Southeast Asia. Gold from Sumatra is thought to have reached as far west as

Rome, while a slave from the Sulu Sea was believed to have been used in Magellan's voyage as a translator.

Originally most people were animist. This was later replaced by Brahmanic Hinduism. Theravada Buddhism soon followed in 525. In 15th century, Islamic influences began to enter. This forced the last Hindu court in Indonesia to retreat to Bali.

In Mainland Southeast Asia, Myanmar, Cambodia and Thailand retained the Theravada form of Buddhism, brought to them from Sri Lanka. This type of Buddhism was fused with the Hindu-influenced Khmer culture.

**Indianized Kingdoms**

Very little is known about Southeast Asian religious beliefs and practices before the advent of Indian merchants and religious influences from the 2nd century BCE onwards. Prior to the 13th century CE, Hinduism and Buddhism were the main religions in Southeast Asia.

The Jawa Dwipa Hindu kingdom in Java and Sumatra existed around 200 BCE. The history of the Malay-speaking world begins with the advent of Indian influence, which dates back to at least the 3rd century BCE. Indian traders came to the archipelago both for its abundant forest and maritime products and to trade with merchants from China, who also discovered the Malay world at an early date. Both Hinduism and Buddhism were well established in the Malay Peninsula by the beginning of the 1st century CE, and from there spread across the archipelago.

Cambodia was first influenced by Hinduism during the beginning of the Funan kingdom. Hinduism was one of the Khmer Empire's official religions. Cambodia is the home to one of the only two temples dedicated to Brahma in the world. Angkor Wat is also a famous Hindu temple of Cambodia. The Champa civilization was located in what is today central Vietnam, and was a highly indianized Hindu Kingdom.

The Majapahit Empire was an Indianized kingdom based in eastern Java from 1293 to around 1500. Its greatest ruler was Hayam Wuruk, whose reign from 1350 to 1389 marked the empire's peak when it dominated other kingdoms in the southern Malay Peninsula, Borneo, Sumatra, and Bali. Various sources such as the Nagarakertagama also mention that its influence spanned over parts of Celebes, the Moluccas islands, and some areas of western Papua, making it the largest empire to ever exist in Southeast Asian history.

The Cholas excelled in maritime activity in both military and the mercantile fields. Their raids of Kedah and the Srivijaya, and their continued commercial contacts with the Chinese Empire, enabled them to influence the local cultures. Many of the surviving examples of the Hindu cultural influence found today throughout the Southeast Asia are the result of the Chola expeditions.

**Islamization of Southeast Asia**

In the 11th century, a turbulent period occurred in the history of Maritime Southeast Asia, the Indian Chola navy crossed the ocean and attacked the Srivijaya kingdom of Sangrama Vijayatungavarman in Kadaram (Kedah), the capital of the powerful maritime kingdom was sacked and the king was taken captive. Along with Kadaram, Pannai in present day Sumatra and Malaiyur and the Malayan peninsula were attacked too. Soon after that, the king of Kedah Phra Ong Mahawangsa became the first ruler to abandon the traditional Hindu faith, and converted to Islam with the Sultanate of Kedah established in year 1136. Samudera Pasai converted to Islam in the year 1267, the King of Malacca Parameswara married with princess of Pasai, the son became the first sultan of Malacca, soon Malacca became the center of Islam study and maritime trade, other rulers followed suit. Indonesian religious leader and Islamic scholar Hamka (1908–1981) wrote in 1961: *"The development of Islam in Indonesia and Malaya is intimately related to a Chinese Muslim, Admiral Zheng He."*

There are several theories to the Islamization process in Southeast Asia. The first theory is trade. The expansion of trade among West Asia, India and Southeast Asia helped the spread of the religion as Muslim traders brought Islam to the region. The second theory is the role of missionaries or Sufis. The Sufi missionaries played a significant role in spreading the faith by syncretising Islamic ideas with existing local beliefs and religious notions. Finally, the ruling classes embraced Islam and that further aided the permeation of the religion throughout the region. The ruler of the region's most important port, Malacca Sultanate, embraced Islam in the 15th century, heralding a period of accelerated conversion of Islam throughout the region as the religion provided a unifying force among the ruling and trading classes.

## Trade and Colonization

### *China*

Chinese merchants have traded with the region for a long time as evidence of Magellan's voyage records that Brunei possessed more cannon than the European ships so it appears that the Chinese fortified them.

Malaysian legend has it that a Chinese Ming emperor sent a princess, Han Li Po, to Malacca, with a retinue of 500, to marry Sultan Mansur Shah after the emperor was impressed by the wisdom of the sultan. Han Li Po's well (constructed 1459) is now a tourist attraction there, as is Bukit Cina, where her retinue settled.

The strategic value of the Strait of Malacca, which was controlled by Sultanate of Malacca in the 15th and early

16th century, did not go unnoticed by Portuguese writer Duarte Barbosa, who in 1500 wrote "He who is lord of Malacca has his hand on the throat of Venice".

***Europe***

Western influence started to enter in the 16th century, with the arrival of the Portuguese and Spanish in Moluccas and the Philippines. Later the Dutch established the Dutch East Indies; the French Indochina; and the British Strait Settlements. All southeast Asian countries were colonized except for Thailand.

European explorers were reaching Southeast Asia from the west and from the east. Regular trade between the ships sailing east from the Indian Ocean and south from mainland Asia provided goods in return for natural products, such as honey and hornbill beaks from the islands of the archipelago.

Europeans brought Christianity allowing Christian missionaries to become widespread. Thailand also allowed Western science and technology to enter its country.

***Japan***

During World War II, the Imperial Japan invaded most of the former western colonies. The Shôwa occupation regime committed violent actions against indigenous civilians such as the Manila Massacre and the implementation of a system of forced labor, such as the one involving 4 to 10 million *romusha* in Indonesia. A later UN report stated that four million people died in Indonesia as a result of famine and forced labour during the Japanese occupation.

***Present***

Most countries in the region enjoy national autonomy. Democratic forms of government and the recognition of human rights are taking root. ASEAN provides a framework for the integration of commerce.

Conflicting territorial and maritime claims continue to exist, including the conflicting claims by Taiwan, China, Vietnam, Malaysia, Brunei and the Philippines over the Spratly Islands.

Geologically, the Indonesian archipelago is one of the most active vulcanological regions in the world. Geological uplifts in the region have also produced some impressive mountains, culminating in Puncak Jaya in Papua, Indonesia at 5,030 metres (16,024 ft), on the island of New Guinea, it is the only place where ice glacier can be found in Southeast Asia. While the second tallest peak is Mount Kinabalu in Sabah, Malaysia on the island of Borneo with a height of 4,101 meters (13,455 ft). The tallest mountain in the Southeast Asia is Hkakabo Razi at 5,967 meters and can be found in northern Burma. The largest archipelago in the world by size is Indonesia (according to the CIA World Factbook)

***Boundaries***

The Australian continent defines a region adjacent to Southeast Asia, which is also politically separated from the countries of Southeast Asia. But a cultural touch point lies between Papua New Guinea and the Indonesian region of Papua and West Papua, which shares the island of New Guinea with Papua New Guinea.

***Climate***

The climate in Southeast Asia is mainly tropical–hot and humid all year round with plentiful rainfall. Southeast Asia has a wet and dry season caused by seasonal shift in winds or monsoon. The tropical rain belt causes additional rainfall during the monsoon season. The rain forest is the second largest on earth (with the Amazon being the largest). An exception to this type of climate and vegetation is the mountain areas in the northern region, where high altitudes lead to milder temperatures and drier landscape. Other parts fall out of this climate because they are desert like.

## Economy

It is pertinent to note that even prior to the penetration of European interests, Southeast Asia was a critical part of the world trading system. The Ryukyu Kingdom often participated in maritime trade in Southeast Asia. A wide range of commodities originated in the region, but especially important were such spices as pepper, ginger, cloves, and nutmeg. The spice trade initially was developed by Indian and Arab merchants, but it also brought Europeans to the region. First Spaniards (Manila galleon) and Portuguese, then the Dutch, and finally the British and French became involved in this enterprise in various countries. The penetration of European commercial interests gradually evolved into annexation of territories, as traders lobbied for an extension of control to protect and expand their activities.

As a result, the Dutch moved into Indonesia, the British into Malaya, the French into Indochina and the Spanish and the U.S. into the Philippines. While the region's economy greatly depends on agriculture, manufacturing and services are becoming more important. An emerging market, Indonesia is the largest economy in this region. Newly industrialized countries including Malaysia, Thailand, and the Philippines while Singapore and Brunei are affluent developed economies. The rest of Southeast Asia is still heavily dependent on agriculture, but Vietnam is notably making steady progress in developing its industrial sectors. The region notably manufactures textiles, electronic high-tech goods such as microprocessors and heavy industrial products such as automobiles. Reserves of oil are also present in the region.

Seventeen telecommunications companies have contracted to build a new submarine cable to connect Southeast Asia to the U.S. This is to avoid disruption of the kind recently caused by the cutting of the undersea cable from Taiwan to the U.S. in a recent earthquake.

Tourism has been a key factor in economic development for many Southeast Asian countries, especially Cambodia. According to UNESCO, "tourism, if correctly conceived, can be a tremendous development tool and an effective means of preserving the cultural diversity of our planet." Since the early 1990s, "even the non-ASEAN nations such as Cambodia, Laos, Vietnam and Burma, where the income derived from tourism is low, are attempting to expand their own tourism industries." In 1995, Singapore was the regional leader in tourism receipts relative to GDP at over 8%. By 1998, those receipts had dropped to less than 6% of GDP while Thailand and Lao PDR increased receipts to over 7%. Since 2000, Cambodia has surpassed all other ASEAN countries and generated almost 15% of its GDP from tourism in 2006.

Indonesia is the only member of G-20 major economies and considered as the largest economy in the region. Indonesia's estimated gross domestic product (nominal) for 2008 was US$511.7 billion with estimated nominal per capita GDP was US$2,246, and per capita GDP PPP was US$3,979 (international dollars).

**Demographics**

Southeast Asia has an area of approximately 4,000,000 km$^2$ (1.6 million square miles). As of 2004, more than 593 million people lived in the region, more than a fifth of them (125 million) on the Indonesian island of Java, the most densely populated large island in the world. Indonesia is the most populous country with 230 million people and also 4th most populous country in the world. The distribution of the religions and people is diverse in Southeast Asia and varies by country. Some 30 million overseas Chinese, not including the heritage, also live in Southeast Asia, most prominently in Christmas Island, Malaysia, the Philippines, Singapore, Indonesia and Thailand, and also, as the Hoa, in Vietnam.

***Ethnic Groups***

According to a recent Stanford genetic study, the Southeast Asian population is far from being homogeneous. Although primarily descendants of Austronesian, Tai, and Mon-Khmer-speaking immigrants who migrated from Southern China during the Bronze Age and Iron Age, there are overlays of Arab, Chinese, Indian, Polynesian and Melanesian genes.

There are also large pockets of intermarriage between indigenous Southeast Asians and those of Chinese descent. They form a substantial part of everyday life in countries such as Vietnam, Singapore, Thailand and the Philippines. Indonesia and Malaysia also has mixed Southeast Asian-Chinese populations.

Remnants of the Mon group are found in parts of Myanmar and Thailand; the ethnic mixture there has been produced by overlaying Tibeto-Burman and Tai, Lao, and Shan peoples. The contemporary Vietnamese population originated from the Red River area in the north and may be a mixture of Tai and Malay peoples. Added to these major ethnic groups are such less numerous peoples as the Karens, Chins, and Nagas in Burma, who have affinities with other Asiatic peoples.

Insular Southeast Asia contains a mixture of descendants of Proto-Malay (Nesiot) and Pareoean peoples who were influenced by Malayo-Polynesian and other groups. In addition, Arabic, Indian, and Chinese influences have affected the ethnic pattern of the islands. Remarkably, modern times, the Javanese are the largest ethnic group in Southeast Asia, with more than 86 million people, mostly concentrated in Java, Indonesia. In Burma, the Burmese account for more than two-thirds of the ethnic stock in this country, while ethnic Thais and Vietnamese account for about four-fifths of the respective populations of those countries.

Indonesia is clearly dominated by the Javanese and Sundanese ethnic groups, while Malaysia is more evenly split between the Malays and the Chinese. Within the Philippines, the Tagalog, Cebuano, Ilocano, and Bicol groups are significant.

### *Religions*

Islam is the most widely practiced religion in Southeast Asia, numbering approximately 240 million adherents which translate to about 40% of the entire population, with majorities in Brunei, Indonesia and Malaysia. Countries in Southeast Asia practice many different religions. Mainland Southeast Asian countries, which are, Thailand, Cambodia, Laos, Burma, Vietnam and Singapore practice predominantly Buddhism. Ancestor worship and Confucianism is also widely practiced in Vietnam and Singapore.

In Maritime Southeast Asia, people living in Malaysia, western Indonesia and Brunei practice mainly Islam. Christianity is predominant in the Philippines because of Spanish colonization for more than 300 years, eastern Indonesia and East Timor. The Philippines has the largest Roman Catholic population followed very distantly by Vietnam. East Timor is also predominantly Roman Catholic due to a history of Portuguese rule.

### *Languages*

Each of the languages have been influenced by cultural pressures due to trade and historical colonization as well. Thus, for example, a Filipino, educated in English and Filipino, as well as in his native tongue (e.g., Visayan), might well speak another language, such as Spanish for historical reasons, or Chinese, Korean or Japanese for economic reasons; a Malaysian might well speak English, Chinese, Tamil as well as Malay as a second language.

The language composition for each country is as follows:

| | |
|---|---|
| Brunei | Malay, English, Chinese, indigenous Borneian dialects |
| Burma | Burmese, Shan, Karen, Rakhine, Kachin, Chin, Mon, Chinese languages, Indian languages, others |
| Cambodia | Khmer, English, French, Vietnamese, Thai, Chamic dialects, Chinese languages, others |
| Christmas Island | English, Chinese, Malay |
| Cocos (Keeling) Islands | English, Cocos Malay |
| East Timor | Tetum, Portuguese, Indonesian, English, Mambae, Makasae, Tukudede, Bunak, Galoli, Kemak, Fataluku, Baikeno, others |
| Indonesia | Indonesian, Hakka, Min Chinese, Cantonese, Acehnese, Batak, Minang, Sundanese, Javanese, Banjarese,Sasak, Tetum, Dayak, Minahasa, Toraja, Buginese, Halmahera, Ambonese, Ceramese; Dutch, Papuan languages, others |
| Laos | Lao, Thai, Vietnamese, Hmong, Miao, Mien, Dao, Shan; French, English others |
| Malaysia | Malay, English, Min Chinese, Hakka, Cantonese, Mandarin, Indian languages, Sarawakian and Sabahan languages, others |
| Philippines | Filipino, English, Minnan Chinese, Tagalog, Cebuano, Ilocano, Hiligaynon/Ilonggo, Kapampangan, Bicol, Waray, Pangasinan, and Arabic (optional) |
| Singapore | English, Mandarin, Malay, Tamil, Min Chinese, Cantonese, Hakka, Shanghainese, other Indian languages, Arabic dialects, others |
| South China Sea Islands | English, Filipino, Malay, Mandarin Chinese, Vietnamese |
| Thailand | Thai, Minnan Chinese, Hakka Chinese, Cantonese, English, Malay, Lao, Khmer, Isaan, Shan, Lue, Phutai, Mon, Mein, Hmong, Karen, Burmese, others |
| Vietnam | Vietnamese, English, Cantonese, Minnanese, French, Khmer, mountain area languages (Mon-Khmer and Malayo-Polynesian, hmong) |

After having a thorough look at southeast Asian region, now we will turn to current changing scenario of Asia-Pacific region, touching all vital concerns and issues.

## REFERENCES

*Chinese Muslims in Malaysia, History and Development,* Rosey Wang Ma

Indonesia—The World Factbook https://www.cia.gov/library/publications/the-world-factbook/geos/id.html

John W. Dower (1986) *War Without Mercy: Race and Power in the Pacific War* (1986; Pantheon.

Library of Congress, 1992, "Indonesia: World War II and the Struggle For Independence, 1942-50; The Japanese Occupation, 1942-45" Access date: February 9, 2007.

Papua New Guinea asks RP support for Asean membership bid Retrieved July 8, 2009

Rand, Nelson (2009). *Conflict: Journeys through war and terror in SouthEast Asia*. Dunboyne: Maverick House Publishers

*Statistics Singapore - Population (Mid Year Estimates) & Land Area*. 2009. Statistics Singapore. 2009. http://www.singstat.gov.sg/stats/keyind.html#popnarea.

Tiwari, Rajnish (2003): *Post-crisis Exchange Rate Regimes in Southeast Asia* (PDF), Seminar Paper, University of Hamburg.

# 2

# Asian-Pacific Region: Changing Scenario

The region of Asia and the Pacific is most impressive in size. It accounts for two thirds of the world population and three fifths of the area of the planet (including land and sea). The characteristics of the region play a central role in the peace and security concerns of the Asian and Pacific nations.

In the era after the World War II, thinking has been dominated by the bipolar confrontation between the United States of America and the Union of Soviet Socialist Republics (since defunct) and its effects on global security or on the national security of individual States. The stress on the role of the major Powers has also led to neglect of the security concerns of medium and small States, except with regard to their importance in the larger strategic context. The security concerns of the States of the Asia and Pacific region can be analysed only in the global strategic context, which, in turn, provides a basis for a regional approach to the settlement of peace and security issues of the region.

It is significant to note that transformation of Marxist systems in the Soviet Union and Eastern Europe reveals once again the force of nationalism, so often the root cause of war in this destructive and tumultuous century. The old order changes: intractable and complex problems remain. Many are as ancient as human society itself: recourse to violence in pursuit of national objectives; the persistence of poverty, famine, disease, injustice, racial and religious intolerance. Others are more recent and the direct consequence of the pace of developments in the modern industrialized world: the weakness of many, perhaps most, modern nation States; the challenges of global climatic change, over-population, industrial pollution and the destruction of the natural environment. Others again are old challenges, made more devastating by modern technology: terrorism, civil strife and revolutionary struggle. Above all, there remains—as what should be the overwhelming preoccupation of the international system—the need to do so much more to achieve a fair and easier life for the vast majority of people.

### The Challenge of Diversity

Geographically along the western rim of the Pacific there is no equivalent of the regional fault that has divided east and west in Europe since 1945. The security equation is dominated by two very different factors. The first, and most potent, factor is the intersection, in the northern part of the region, of great-Power interests and strategic concerns on the part of the four most powerful countries in the world—China, Japan, the Russia and the United States of America. The second factor is the perpetuation, in different parts of the region, of ancient enmities, linked sometimes with religious or ideological fervour, or exacerbated by differences between rich and poor and—often enough—by the intervention of outside Powers.

The mosaic of Asian-Pacific nations is made up of many nationalities and cultures; the geography is disparate and difficult; most significant of all, in terms of the security preoccupations of the region, power is unevenly spread. The single most striking feature is diversity.

In terms of per capita wealth, another perspective emerges. Nauru is one of the wealthiest countries in the world, with a gross domestic product per head of $A 21,400.

In Singapore, wealth per capita was $US 12,626. Such statistics are hardly a satisfactory measure of relative weight or of the security issues within the Asian-Pacific region. They certainly cannot measure quality of life or other major factors involved in the security equations. They do no more than underscore the diversity of the Western Pacific and the wide range of national entities which must be taken into account in any attempt to come to terms with the concerns of individual countries.

What is more, this year's events in the region have taken, in some respects, the opposite course from that charted in Europe. The miserable struggle of the Cambodian people for internal order and decency goes on and on. Refugees from Indochina, whether displaced by war or in hope of some relief from a harsh and threadbare existence, continue to flood the resettlement camps. In Myanmar, repression and the restoration of military power have followed the high expectations of reform generated in 1988. In the Philippines, the Government of President Aquino has been assailed by a further military coup. The framework for authority in Manila is now weak and the Government must proceed with caution. In attempting to bring guerrilla insurgency under control it is challenged by anti-communist forces, ostensibly because it is dealing with the terrorists.

## Regional Groupings for Mutual Cooperation

In fact, as regards groupings, the Asian-Pacific world is in transition. There is no long history of regionalism and there are no institutions capable of bringing together the many-sided elements in the regional equation. Few now recall the Asian and Pacific Council (ASPAC), an initiative taken by a grouping of nine countries of the region during the 1960s to meet regularly to try to develop a (generally anti-communist) focus on matters of common political and security concern. With neither a strong sense of homogeneity nor experience of working together the participants found that such an arrangement lacked the necessary strength to cope with the intricacies of the region. It was evident also that at that time, with the Viet Nam War the major issue, major-Power preoccupations were dominant. At a subregional level, the Association of South-East Asian Nations (ASEAN) has become, in the course of almost thirty years, a principal element in the foreign policies of Indonesia, Malaysia, the Philippines, Singapore and Thailand—with Brunei Darussalam a more recent member. ASEAN has served as a means of concerting national points of view and promoting common interests, particularly in matters of economic collaboration and development assistance. Most important perhaps, the Association has served as a sounding-board for many of the concerns of the region, particularly in respect of Indochina. It is a measure of the respect that ASEAN has attained that major external Powers—the United States, Japan, Australia, New Zealand, Canada and the European Community—attach importance to their status as dialogue partners of the ASEAN group—so much so that they are almost invariably represented by senior ministers at the annual discussion meetings of ASEAN.

Similarly, the South Pacific Forum, established in 1971, is another important subregional grouping, comprising the island States of the Pacific plus Australia and New Zealand. Annual meetings are held to consider the issues facing the region and to plan regional co-operative programmes to meet some of the particular difficulties in trade, transport and communications, and matters relating to fishing and the law of the sea, which face the often small Pacific Island countries.

The questions of decolonization and nuclear testing within the region, and the onset of marked instability in some parts of the Pacific, have also claimed the attention of Forum countries. The Forum has established specialist secretariats, for example the South Pacific Bureau for Economic Cooperation and the Forum Fisheries Agency, to co-ordinate efforts in certain fields. The Forum also provides a focus for outside Powers with interests in the region, which have now been invited to an annual discussion meeting. In 1989 an initiative of the Australian Prime Minister to promote a wider association of Pacific rim countries for the purpose of co-ordinating economic and development interests began to bear fruit. A meeting was held at Canberra early in November, at which it was agreed to proceed further with exploring practical measures of economic co-operation. The new grouping has been tentatively called Asia Pacific Economic Cooperation (APEC).

It is worthy to mention that whereas in other regions of the world—Africa and Latin America—there are single institutions capable of providing a focus for the concerns of regional States, no such concentration of interests has yet been possible in Asia and the Pacific. The contrast with Europe is even more marked. While the coherence of Eastern Europe is changing, its economies still have much in common. In Western Europe, the European Community derives strength from its political institutions, legal processes, and far-reaching programmes of economic and agricultural co-operation. The Asian Development Bank is one regional agency in the Western Pacific that has a mandate to promote economic progress; however, in the absence of the Russia, Viet Nam and China, its membership is hardly representative of the region. Business/ governmental organizations such as the Pacific Economic Cooperation Council provide some further coherence for economic interests.

Besides recent emergence of India and China as global economic giants, in view of the phenomenon which is present-day Japan and the associated rapid economic progress of the Asian new industrial countries—the Republic of Korea, Hong Kong and Singapore, with Thailand generally reckoned to be the most recent addition—the region is a driving force in the world economy. It appears too that the success of these countries is contagious. Indonesia and Malaysia follow close behind the leading members of the group of so-called

Asian "tigers". What were regarded, not so long ago, as developing countries are showing the way to solid economic progress associated with noteworthy political stability and a growing sense of national confidence. Within the span of 20 years this process had dramatically changed the geopolitical map. The archipelagos and islands of the Western Pacific are no longer an uninterrupted zone of instability and under-development. Sources of insecurity deriving from political discontent and ideological struggle are gradually vanishing. There has been no territorial aggrandizement or assertion of military power behind the startling economic progress of the region. Nor has the leap forward of these remarkable countries been a consequence of the exploitation of their own sources of mineral wealth. Rather they have achieved spectacular economic growth by harnessing the industrial techniques of the modern age to the opportunities of an increasingly free international industrial trading system.

## Regional Security Issues

There remain serious regional security issues and challenges. In Indo-China, the fighting has flowed across international borders. Even there, however, the Soviet Union has exercised influence in achieving the withdrawal from Cambodia of Vietnamese forces. However, inability to agree at an international level on a regime acceptable to all contending parties has meant that the long and bitter travail of the Khmer people continues. Territorial disputes over the islands and reefs in the South China Sea have led to military confrontation between China and Viet Nam; Malaysia and the Philippines are also claimants with strong interests. The dispute between Japan and the Soviet Union over Soviet occupation, in the last days of the World War II, of four small islands to the north of Hokkaido continues to be a major impediment to constructive relations between these two major regional Powers. The border between China and Viet Nam has been the cause of major fighting in recent years, while that between China and the Soviet Union along the Amur River has periodically raised levels of tension in the region.

In South-East Asia, Thailand has been in military confrontation with Laos over border alignments; while Malaysia and the Philippines have, it seems, resolved longstanding differences about their respective boundary lines to the north of Sabah. The border between Papua New Guinea and Indonesia is in effect a major global boundary between the Pacific and the Asian worlds. As such it has been the scene of military activity on both sides to keep a check on the flow of people across what is an ill-defined line in difficult country. The presence of foreign military bases and/or other military installations is an irritant to sectors of political opinion in several countries. In the changed relationships between the Soviet Union and the United States, the continuation of their bases in Viet Nam and the Philippines has become increasingly uncertain. Direct super-Power involvement in South-East Asia may well come to be seen, sooner rather than later, as no longer required or appropriate. All of the ASEAN countries now have their own effective military capabilities; all maintain an intense interest in the strategic waterway which bisects the region.

The strategic relationship of the United States with Japan is however far from being a thing of the past. Any abrupt, unplanned changes in the present subtle balance of interests would be a cause for global concern. Change can nevertheless be expected as the global alliance system is reconsidered in the light of shifts in the strategic balance elsewhere. In this context, the interactions between the major Powers—in the north-west of the region—remain delicately poised. There is nothing immutable about the respective positions of the Powers involved—particularly when set against the forces of regionalism and nationalism now at work in the Soviet Union and, it seems, in China.

The same considerations apply to the animus that marks the relationship between the Democratic People's Republic of Korea and the Republic of Korea at the 38th parallel. The new-found wealth of Taiwan and the recent tragic failure to find a political balance in the People's Republic of China decrease the chances for peaceful settlement of the burning issue of reconciliation between the two. Political stability in the Philippines has proved elusive and insurgency remains a serious threat. The sorry civil strife in Myanmar has locked that country back in on itself. Indonesian reconciliation with independence movements in East Timor and Irian Jaya is, by now the complete. In the South Pacific, military coups in Fiji, riots in Vanuatu, threats of secession in Papua New Guinea, violent confrontations in New Caledonia, an act of terrorism by French officials in New Zealand, and concerns about external meddling in some small island States have shattered illusions of a calm and sequestered part of the world.

The picture is therefore dominated by the dynamic economic advance of several countries, but this must be balanced against the many challenging and all too often tragic manifestations of political and social pressures which cannot yet be accommodated. There is no reason however for concern about major challenges to the existing balance of power in the region, such as occurred before and during the World War II.

While the overall picture in Asia and the Pacific is now encouraging, the recent history has been one of deep divisions and painful struggle. The anti-colonial impetus has largely been removed. It is nevertheless clear that many security concerns are not superficial and will not readily be smoothed over. The region has been, for a number of years, the arena for the contest between conflicting ideologies. Regional revolutionary struggle thus became enmeshed in the larger confrontation between major global interests, so much so that the South-East Asian region became a by-word for instability and dislocation. Around the entire rimlands of the Eurasian continent, struggles for national self-determination against established colonial regimes broke out at the conclusion of the World War II.

The travails of the South-East Asian and wider Asian regions have been many and costly. For many years it appeared that the region would, for a long time to come, be beset by tumult and political instability. Concerns about security extended beyond the immediate region to influence the attitudes and policies of Australia and New Zealand, both countries with vested interests in stability and constructive development in the whole broad zone of the western Pacific. Great-Power preoccupations focused not only on the outcome of the ideological struggle in the area, but on the strategic importance of preserving a balance of power, particularly in relation to the vital trade routes traversing the region. Against the evidence of a turbulent recent history, there will clearly continue to be widespread and continuing sensitivity to the complexity and inherent difficulties of this part of the world.

It is remarkable to note that the political and military back-cloth to the successful disarmament initiatives taken in Europe is simply not present in Asia. So far it has been possible to achieve some limited progress only by way of an adjunct to the agreements on major weapons systems in the European theatre. Thus the Western side sought to ensure that intermediate-range missiles would not just be transferred to Asian targets when a global limit of 100 missiles was set for each side in the Treaty on the Elimination of Intermediate-Range and Shorter-Range Missiles adopted in 1987. Further development of that agreement to eliminate these classes of weapons entirely has of course removed this question from super-Power calculations in Asia. China and the Soviet Union have succeeded in reaching agreement on major reductions in ground forces deployed along their common border. For both parties the issue has been less the attainment of balanced security at lower levels of forces than a response to other pressing domestic considerations.

China in particular is making impressive reductions in overall troop strengths. The aim however has been to reshape the People's Liberation Army as a more modern and leaner force, better equipped and more mobile than the previous mass army. Russia for its part had seen redeployment away from the Chinese border as an important means of reducing defence costs.

The interests of the principal Asian-Pacific actors are also changing, so that strategic confrontation is being blurred. Japan has become the major economic partner of China; the United States is concerned to preserve the openness of China to the West; Russia has staked its irrefutable claims as a Pacific Power; there are powerful interests in Russia in the promotion of economic linkages with Japan. There is no longer any clear demarcation of ideology, let alone of strategic or economic interests. In the absence of effective regional institutions, careful and balanced statecraft is required and that in turn calls for openness and understanding, qualities which are, it seems, difficult to develop after many years of suspicion and hostility.

Arms control in the Asian-Pacific region must also start from the fact of a notable increase in the acquisition of modern weapons systems by South-East Asian countries. Policies of self-reliance and independence demand nothing less. Regional and subregional approaches certainly offer possibilities. The South Pacific Nuclear Free Zone Treaty is predicated on this principle. The Treaty has given South Pacific countries the opportunity to declare their commitment to renunciation of the acquisition, manufacture, stationing or testing of nuclear explosive devices. The area of the Treaty joins to the east the zone of application of the Treaty for the Prohibition of Nuclear Weapons in Latin America. To the south the Treaty area abuts on that of the Antarctic Treaty, which has long provided for exclusion of nuclear testing and the banning of military activity. The concept of a zone of peace, freedom and neutrality in South-East Asia has been given earnest consideration by the ASEAN members. Australia has taken an important initiative in focusing international attention on the need to reinforce and bring up to date existing international provisions for banning chemical weapons.

There are hopes in the international community that it will prove possible for the big-Powers to extend their agreements about intermediate-range nuclear missiles on land to similar sea-borne weapons systems. So far however there is little incentive to promote such concepts in the Asian-Pacific region. The strategic issues are perhaps less pressing than the regional. At that level too, however, history is against rapid progress.

The Asian-Pacific region has its own dynamism. It is plainly not immune to the sweeping changes in the global order that have had their origins in recent events in Europe. At the same time, it is itself rapidly developing and moving away from a recent turbulent history. Security concerns for all the countries of the region are nevertheless bound to be shaped to a large extent by experience of that stormy past. Above all, it will be recalled that the catastrophe of all-out war in the Asian-Pacific region during the years from 1935 to 1945 was not confined to the immediate area of Japan. The maritime character of much of the region, together with the interpenetration of interests of most if not all of its member countries, ensures a wide sharing of strategic-concerns.

The most pervasive danger would plainly arise should the complex balance of forces of the region again be disturbed by one of the major Powers seeking to pursue its objectives by military means. There is however no such prospect in view. Moreover, intra-regional challenges to the established order appear to be lessening. There remain many sources of tension. Fighting goes on and many lives are continuing to be blighted in the process. The fact that the struggles of the region—however regrettable in themselves—are now mainly at the lower end of the military spectrum offers hope, at least, that it will be possible to bring such tragedies as Cambodia under control, perhaps by collective action under the auspices of the United Nations. That in itself would be a new step for the region and a cause for further optimism for the future.

## Asia and the Pacific

The problem of peace and security in Asia and the Pacific is similar to that in Europe and the whole world. However, this region has special characteristics of its own. Forty-five years ago, all countries in this region—except the Soviet Union, the United States and Japan—were colonies or semi-colonies of Western Powers. The most striking feature of the situation was and is the struggle for freedom of all peoples in the area and their achievement of political independence through different means, peaceful or military. The coming into existence of the Republic of India and the People's Republic of China, the victorious armed struggle of the peoples of Indonesia, Viet Nam, Laos and Cambodia, among others, have added glorious pages to the history of national liberation movements and have altered the political map of this region. It is noteworthy that during the same period there has been no modification whatsoever of the map of Europe. In spite of a bitter cold war, a state of peaceful co-existence between the two groupings of nations with different political and social systems has, in fact, prevailed.

In 1954, India and China advanced the five principles of peaceful co-existence, the Panchasheel. The 1955 Afro-Asian Conference held at Bandung, Indonesia, laid the foundation of solidarity among Asian, African and Latin American peoples in their struggle for independence and freedom and led to the founding of the Movement of Non-Aligned Countries in 1961. The rising tide of peace, national independence and non-alignment in the region paralysed and then wiped out such military alliances as the South-East Asia Treaty Organization and the Central Treaty Organization.

Today, peace and development have characterized the prevailing trends in the Asian and Pacific area. Mongolia's proposal for the establishment of a mechanism for the non-use of force in relations among countries in Asia and the Pacific has been widely supported. The increasing endeavours of the hinterland and littoral States to convene the International Conference on the Indian Ocean heralds their contribution to the promotion of peace and security in the region. The Soviet statement at Vladivostok and the Indo-Soviet New Delhi statement have expressed the desire of the Asian-Pacific nations for peace and have charted a practical way to attain regional peace and security.

As the first victims of the atomic bomb, the people of Asia and the Pacific are also among the fiercest opponents of the use of nuclear weapons in their region or elsewhere in the world. In this respect, Japan has proposed three nuclear-free principles, and thousands of cities and towns in that country have declared themselves nuclear-free. With the Treaty of Rarotonga, the South Pacific has become a nuclear-free zone and there is now a growing tendency among South-East Asian countries to follow suit. Of the three nuclear Powers in Asia and the Pacific, the Soviet Union and China have committed themselves never to be the first to use nuclear weapons.

At the same time, most countries in Asia and the Pacific are making every effort to get rid of poverty and backwardness, and are striving for economic development; this is one of the main factors motivating them to safeguard peace, security and stability in the region together with their own independence and freedom. According to data provided by the Economic and Social Commission for Asia and the Pacific, there are as many as 510 million people in this region living in poverty—89 per cent of the poverty-stricken population of the world. The demand for economic development is now a driving force making this region the most dynamic in the world. This dynamism reveals itself in the high rate of progress recorded by India, Indonesia, Hong Kong, Singapore, the Republic of Korea, Taiwan and some other countries. The new stage of the scientific and technological revolution that began in the 1970s will bring about achievements of decisive significance in different fields in decades to come.

> Socialist Republic of Viet Nam made public its four-point policy towards its neighbours in South-East Asia:
>
> a. Respect for one another's independence, sovereignty and territorial integrity, non-aggression, non-intervention in one another's affairs, equality and mutual benefit;
>
> b. Solution of all disputes among countries in the area through peaceful means, without foreign interference;
>
> c. Non-participation in any military alliance and refusal to allow its territory to be used against neighbouring countries in the region;
>
> d. Co-existence with one another in peace, friendship and co-operation, and the conversion of South-East Asia into a zone of peace, independence and neutrality.

We fully share President Suharto's concept of national and regional resilience and hold the view that all regional matters must be solved by the countries of the region without interference from outside. In the mid-1980s, Viet Nam declared its readiness to adhere to ZOPFAN and the Bali Treaty and favoured the establishment of a nuclear-weapon-free zone in our region. In 1988, the Lao People's Democratic Republic, on its own behalf and on behalf of the People's Republic of Kampuchea and the Socialist Republic of Viet Nam proposed establishing a zone of peace, freedom, neutrality, friendship and co-operation in South-East Asia.

## The Problem of Cambodia

In fact Cambodia has long been an area of tension in South-East Asia, a fact that has been attributed by some to the presence of Vietnamese volunteer troops in Cambodia. Unless the subject is clearly understood, no real solution will be possible.

The Cambodian question goes back to the extermination in the "killing fields" of 3 million Cambodians at the hands of the genocidal Pol Pot regime. At that time, worldwide indignation at the atrocities reached its climax. Public opinion and many statesmen joined in recommending that troops from the third world be dispatched urgently to Cambodia to overthrow the genocidal regime and save the Cambodian people, as had been done in the case of certain other brutal regimes.

In 1979 the Vietnamese volunteer troops were sent to Cambodia to fight alongside the Cambodian people against the genocidal clique. Three years later, as the rebirth of the Cambodian people was making progress, Viet Nam began withdrawing part of its forces on a yearly basis, until they were pulled out completely by 26 September 1989.

The two Jakarta Informal Meetings (JIM), held in July 1988 and February 1989 respectively, created the necessary conditions, internationally, for the Cambodian parties to enter into talks with a view to finding a solution to the internal aspect. On the basis of the talks between the two sides in Cambodia and of the conclusions of the two Jakarta Informal Meetings, the International Conference on Cambodia was held in Paris from 30 July to 30 August 1989 under the co-presidency of France and Indonesia. Although a few substantial differences still remain, the Paris Conference agreed on many important issues and laid the groundwork for an early, comprehensive political settlement of the Cambodian problem. It is generally accepted that the momentum generated by the Paris Conference must be maintained and that the initial results must be built upon further if lasting peace and stability in Cambodia and in all of South-East Asia are to be restored in the near future.

The Paris Conference did in fact reach an agreement on all the fundamental and long-term issues of an over-all solution to the Cambodian problem, namely: total withdrawal of Vietnamese troops from Cambodia; non-return to power of the genocidal regime in Cambodia; cessation of foreign military aid to the Cambodian parties; respect for the independence, sovereignty, neutrality and non-alignment of Cambodia; implementation of the Cambodian people's right to self-determination through free, fair and democratic general elections; an international guarantee of the agreements and the setting up of a body, the International Control Mechanism (ICM), for supervision of the implementation of the agreements.

Two issues remain outstanding. The first is the setting up of a provisional authority with the task of holding general elections in the transitional period between the total pull-out of Vietnamese troops and the general elections. The second is the United Nations role in the International Control Mechanism.

As for the role of the United Nations, there is a point that needs to be spelt out here. Viet Nam does not object to—indeed it even welcomes—a United Nations role in a Cambodian settlement and in an international control mechanism in Cambodia, provided however that the United Nations takes a fair and impartial attitude towards the Cambodian issue.

Viet Nam has more than once expressed its appreciation of the personal efforts made by the Secretary-General of the United Nations to encourage dialogue aimed at a political solution to the Cambodian question. At the Paris Conference, Cambodia and Viet Nam approved from the very beginning the Secretary-General's proposal with regard to dispatching a fact-finding mission to Cambodia.

It is our hope that the United Nations will adopt such a fair and impartial stand in keeping with the positive developments embodied in the JIMs, the talks between the two Cambodian sides, the Paris Conference on Cambodia and the summit meetings of the non-aligned countries and will therefore play a major role in this regard.

After the total withdrawal of Vietnamese troops from Cambodia in September 1989, the upsurge of the fighting among the Cambodian parties has given rise to general concern all over the world regarding the threat of a return to power of the Khmer Rouge. Many initiatives and proposals have been set forth in an attempt to prevent civil war and the recurrence of the genocidal Pol Pot regime and to promote the search for a solution. Among those initiatives are the proposal made on 23 September 1989 by the Prime Minister of Thailand, His Excellency Mr. Chatichai Choonhavan, for a cease-fire in Cambodia and the convening of an informal meeting to discuss the setting up of an international mechanism with a mandate to verify Vietnamese troop withdrawal and to supervise the cease-fire and the cessation of all foreign arms supply to all parties in Cambodia; and the joint statement of 23 September 1989 by the United States and the Soviet Union regarding a moratorium on military assistance to all Cambodian factions. Most recently, the Australian Foreign Minister, His Excellency Mr. Gareth Evans, made a proposal regarding a United Nations-controlled interim administration in Cambodia during the transition period between the withdrawal of Vietnamese troops and the holding of free, fair and democratic general elections. This would necessarily involve having the Cambodian seat in the United Nations currently occupied by Democratic Kampuchea left vacant.

# 3

# South-East Asian Security Issues and Confidence-building

In the present chapter we will present a vivid account of main security concerns in the southeast Asian region. The some concerns today may become irrelevant tomorrow, this narrative will give you a historical development of the issues.

## Main Security Concerns

It is pertinent to note that security issues in the South-East Asian subregion are both diverse and complex, involving as they do some issues that are bilateral and some that are multilateral as well as some that relate both to States of the region and to external actors. For purposes of analysis, the security issues relevant to South-East are dealt with at three levels, although each is not exclusive of the others.

### 1. Great-Power Linkages

First, one level of concern in South-East Asia has been the linkages with the great Powers or their penetration into the security problems of the region. In the bipolar world, the super-Power competition at the global level was projected onto the region. Whether for the Viet Nam war or the Cambodian conflict, South-East Asia provided the arena for the great Powers' conflict and competition.

After cessation of cold war, there have been changes in great-Power relations, characterized by a shift away from confrontation to co-operation, marked by the Sino-Soviet normalization of relations in April 1989; the Conference on Security and Co-operation in Europe (CSCE) held in Paris in November 1990; and, particularly, of direct relevance to South-East Asia, the agreement by the permanent members of the United Nations Security Council on the framework for a settlement of the Cambodian conflict.

The erstwhile Soviet Union unilaterally removed most of its offensive aircraft and naval vessels from Cam Rahn Bay, in line with its new strategic doctrine, which emphasizes a defensive posture. While the United States has announced its intention to remain a major Pacific Power, a reduction of its forces in the area appears inevitable.

The prognosis for a United States base in the Philippines is one of phasing out over a period of from five to ten years, and the recent agreement with Singapore would suggest that the future structure of a United States military presence in the region will be in the nature of a diversified and limited use of facilities. Diplomatically, there have been improvements in relations between the great Powers and the regional States across old adversarial boundaries.

Most dramatic has been China's normalization of relations with Indonesia, which will lead to China's having diplomatic relations with all members of the Association of South-East Asian Nations (ASEAN). China's relations with Laos have been on the upswing. Russia has been pursuing a policy of "constructive engagement" with countries members of ASEAN, the success of which can be gauged by the numerous exchanges of visits by high-ranking officials of both sides. There has been a tentative improvement of relations between China and Viet Nam and between the United States and Viet Nam.

## 2. Main Actors in the Region

Despite the waning of bipolarity, it is expected that South-East Asia will see a greater number of actors in the region, with undefined security implications. Of the utmost concern for South-East Asian countries is China, whose land and sea frontiers border on the region. China is, without a doubt, part of the South-East Asian "security complex" by reason of its close involvement in the Cambodian conflict through support of the resistance, particularly the Khmer Rouge; its border conflict with Viet Nam: and its extensive claim in the South China Sea, which overlaps with the waters of many South-East Asian countries.

With its evident readiness to enforce its claim by force and its formidable military capabilities in local offensive operations, as in the case of the Spratlys, a result of its navy's growing blue water capability, China looms large in the threat perceptions of regional countries. While it can be expected that China will be more militarily assertive in the South China Sea in view of its growing capability, this could be constrained in the short and medium term by its preoccupation with domestic problems and its concern with improving international political and economic relations, including those with ASEAN countries.

Remarkably, major actor of note in South-East Asia is Japan, whose predominance in the economic realm is accompanied by a greater readiness to play a political role commensurate with its economic status. With regard to South-East Asia, Japan has evinced a readiness to play a constructive role in the resolution of the Cambodian conflict, which included an offer to help finance peace keeping and the hosting of a meeting among the Khmer factions in Tokyo in 1990, moves that were generally welcomed in South-East Asia. However, the possibility that Japanese may play a military role in the region is proving to be of concern to most countries in the region as was evident in the negative reaction to the Thai Prime Minister's reported—but later denied—invitation to Japan early in 1990 to hold a joint naval exercise with Thailand.

The major concern in South-East Asia is not so much

Japan's growing military capability as the possibility that Japan might take an independent military role outside of the United States-Japanese security arrangement. Reasons for this concern arise from the growing tensions in United States-Japanese relations and the widening debate in Japan regarding the validity of the United States-Japanese Security Pact.

This concern is, however, of a longer-term nature, discounting the possibility of a precipitous withdrawal of the United States forward deployment from the region, which appears unlikely.

In the present age of globalisation, India is emerging as a giant economic and military power in South Asian region. In a unipolar world India's presence in different world and regional fora cannot be simply ignored. India is another major actor which is beginning to figure in South-East Asia's security consciousness. With the significant advances made by the Indian navy in the 1980s, and the possibility of India's strategic domain eventually extending to South-East Asia, as suggested by some Indian defence analysts, some South-East Asians are beginning to see India as possibly coming within the region's "security complex". This is supplemented by the continuing Sino-Indian conflict and competition. The growing Chinese capability for the projection of its naval power into the Indian Ocean, as suggested by the 1985 South Asia expedition by Chinese warships, and the recent reported Chinese-Myanmar arms deal, provide grounds for speculation over a possible spill-over of the Sino-India competition and conflict into South-East Asia.

Remarkably, at the domestic level, South-East Asian countries are concerned with threats to their internal stability. At a minimum, governments are concerned that their people should be provided with such economic and social welfare as will continue to provide legitimacy for the government. This task is, however, proving to be difficult despite the successes in some countries in producing high growth rates. With few exceptions, there is a trade-off between growth and equity, threatening stability with unmet rising expectations.

Another economic problem is that of maintaining sustained growth when national economies are integrated into the world economy and subjected to the vagaries of the latter. Yet another challenge to the sustaining of economic growth has to do with the depletion of natural resources within a country's own borders. This concern is having an effect on relations among States in the region as each becomes more determined to guard its own resources.

### 3. Intra-Regional Security Concern

The third level of security issues is intra-regional, although external actors are also involved directly or indirectly in a number of issues. The most prominent has to do with disputes over boundaries, both land and sea, which have resulted in armed confrontations and conflicts.

Regionally, disputes over land borders exist between Thailand and Cambodia, Thailand and Laos, Viet Nam and Cambodia. The last two disputes have caused armed clashes in the recent past. More extensive disputes have to do with maritime boundaries. The "new ocean regime", resulting from the Conference on the Law of the Sea, has extended coastal State control over the continental shelf and a 200-mile exclusive economic zone, with a greatly increased incentive for States to establish their sovereignty over islands. Of the 15 possible maritime boundaries in the South China Sea, excluding the Gulf of Thailand, 12 are disputed.

The disputes involve China with Brunei, Malaysia, Indonesia, the Philippines and Viet Nam; and Viet Nam with China, Indonesia, Malaysia and the Philippines. Disputes also exist among ASEAN members, with Malaysia having disputes with all other members. Thailand has disputes also with Cambodia and Viet Nam in the Gulf of Thailand.

However, the dispute that has the greatest potential for armed conflict revolves around the conflicting claims over the Spratly Islands, which include China, Taiwan province of China, Viet Nam, Malaysia and the Philippines, all of which occupy a number of islands. Following the violent eruption of conflict between Chinese and Vietnamese troops in March 1988, disputants appear more ready to protect their claims against future intrusion. For domestic reasons already mentioned, nations are more determined than ever to guard their off-shore resources, which include hydrocarbon, minerals and fisheries. Apart from their existing and potential resources, the Spratlys in particular are also of strategic importance to external Powers, including the United States, Japan and the Soviet Union, as regards the safety of sea-lines of communication. Recently, Chinese Prime Minister Li Peng expressed readiness to joint efforts with South-East Asian countries to develop the Spratly Islands, while putting aside for the time being the question of sovereignty. However, Viet Nam, which is the main contestant, will not be included until relations with China are normalized. This would leave an important gap in conflict management on the Spratlys.

While off-shore resources and the conflict that they entail may be most threatening to the region's security, other resource-related issues with potential for conflict, namely the use of the Mekong River and the exploitation of timber on mainland South-East Asia, should also be taken into consideration.

A potential for intra-regional conflict related to economic issues could arise from the emerging economic interdependence between the more advanced economies and less developed economies in the region. Conflict could arise if there was an unacceptable inequity in the relationship.

Another security issue at the intra-regional level has to do with external support or intervention in armed rebellions in regional countries for ethnic, religious or ideological reasons. Problems with their Muslim minorities in Thailand and the Philippines have caused concern regarding assistance from their kith and kin in neighbouring countries, particularly Malaysia. Laos and Viet Nam have complained about resistance movements allegedly launched from Thailand. Should the Cambodian conflict be settled in such away that the Khmer Rouge continue to carry on an armed struggle against the Phnom Penh regime, problems could arise between Thailand and neighbouring Cambodia.

Much concern has been expressed about the growth in arms procurement in ASEAN countries as a sign of a possible arms race, entailing greater tension and instability in the region. A question that is often raised is why there is this growth while the region's security environment is becoming more benign with the drawing down of the superpowers' military presence and the Vietnamese troop withdrawal from Cambodia. A number of explanations may be given. The first is that of threat perception. The evolving and thus uncertain strategic scenario appears potentially troublesome, with more actors and a lack of clearly defined security threats as well as the felt need to compensate for the perceived drawing down of the United States presence. It is to be noted that the present trend in arms build-up in South-East Asia is characterized by a shift from a doctrine of counter-insurgency to one of conventional warfare. The original impetus to this shift was Viet Nam's invasion of Cambodia. A more recent one is the threat perception in the South China Sea. Because of the focus on maritime defence needs, most ASEAN countries are in the process of upgrading, in particular, their naval and air capabilities. The past positive correlation between the defence spending and the economic health of the country also helps to explain the upward trend in defence expenditure.

Defence spending is following an upward trend also because the existing arsenal of the ASEAN countries is aging and rapidly approaching obsolescence. Further impetus is provided by the existing state of the arms market, which belongs to the buyers owing to a number of factors. It is possible for buyers to diversify their sources of arms supply, to demand easy-payment terms, off-set manufacturing contracts, licensed production of equipment and greater access to technology through co-production and co-development of military hardware. In the case of Thailand, the domestic power equation proves to be an important determinant in the acquisition of arms. Thailand's suspicion of Viet Nam's long-term intentions and Singapore's experience with separation from Malaysia are some of the cases that readily come to mind. When discussing security issues at the intra-regional level, the existing suspicions that nations hold with regard to one another, derived from historical experience, of the distant or the recent past, will continue to figure in relations among them and shape their security perspective.

## ZOPFAN and SEANWFZ

The drawing-down of the two super-Powers' military presence from the region and the expected diminution of their linkages in the region's security problems can be seen as contributing to the realization of a zone of peace, freedom and neutrality (ZOPFAN). However, if we were to look at its origin and the reasons why it has remained basically a goal to be achieved since it was declared in 1971, an answer might be found to the question of its feasibility at present. Originally, when ASEAN was founded, the security of its members was to be attained by the establishment of a regional order in which conflicts among member countries were to be confined and positive co-operation encouraged. In view of its limited resources, protection from external threat was to be provided by the United States. The prospect of the United States moving out of South-East Asia led to the idea of ZOPFAN, which would replace the protection from an external Power by the management of the regional order by the regional States themselves. Underpinning ZOPFAN would be political stability and internal security or national resilience, in Indonesian parlance, which would, in turn, bring about regional resilience by pre-empting external Powers from intervening in domestic or regional affairs.

ZOPFAN's strategy for peace and security through detachment and self-reliance foundered on the reluctance of some members to dispense with external guarantees, and the goal of removing foreign bases was agreed upon without a time-limit being set. The prerequisite of a favourable constellation of external Powers was also lacking. Viet Nam's invasion of Cambodia in December 1978 soon reflected that Power constellation when South-East Asia became clearly polarized.

The present evolving security environment, both at the super-Power level and at the intra-regional level, the latter with the prospect of resolution of the Cambodian conflict and improving relations between ASEAN and the Indochinese countries, appears to fit into the scheme of ZOPFAN. However, judging by the lack of objection by other ASEAN members to Singapore's agreement with the United States in November 1990 providing the latter's warships and planes with greater access of its facilities, at least once they were assured that no permanent basing was involved, indicates the view that the United States presence is benign and stabilizing at the present time of an uncertain and evolving pattern of power.

Nevertheless, the idea of SEANWFZ was first introduced as a stopgap measure for the suspended ZOPFAN. It was to provide a forum at which all South-East Asian countries, then polarized by the Cambodian conflict, could have positive interaction. Assuming that the Cambodian conflict will be resolved in the foreseeable future, consultation on SEANWFZ could provide one venue for integration of Indo-China and Myanmar into a unified South-East Asia. Taking into consideration the United States objection, a piecemeal approach to establishing a nuclear-weapon-free zone (NWFZ) could be chosen over a comprehensive one, which means an agreement in a full-fledged legal instrument that would form the foundation of the denuclearization of the region concerned. In a piecemeal approach, members could start from one of the three essential elements in a NWFZ, namely non-possession. Non-possession is in line with non-proliferation.

This should be easily acceptable, as all except Myanmar and Brunei are signatories of the 1968 Treaty on the Non-Proliferation of Nuclear Weapons. Non-use would follow naturally, leaving non-deployment untouched for the time being. However, judging from the United States position on the NWFZ in the South Pacific, it is even doubtful whether the piecemeal approach would be acceptable to Washington. None the less, ZOPFAN and SEANWFZ remain on the ASEAN agenda and, at the least, they are useful as guides to the enhancement of regional peace and security over the longer term.

## Enhancing and Broadening the ASEAN Process

It is pertinent to note that if confidence-building is defined in a broad sense to mean any measure that builds confidence, then ASEAN has, for a long time, been a confidence-building regime. The formation of ASEAN itself came about with the common realization that confrontation and conflicts that existed among the countries in the region in the past were counter-productive and that security could best be guaranteed by the establishment of a regional order which promoted conflict avoidance and positive co-operation. In a concrete form, the Treaty of Amity and Cooperation in South-East Asia and the Declaration of ASEAN Concord of 1976 laid down the rules of conduct for members by which they would refrain from threatening one another and would settle their disagreements peacefully and without outside interference.

ASEAN can be described as a "security community" in the sense that these rules of conduct have come to be accepted by members. The practice of consultation and consensus-building has reinforced the process of conflict avoidance. Co-operative efforts in political, economic, social and cultural fields also help build a sense of community. All these add up to confidence-building in a comprehensive sense, apart from the politico-military situation. However, questions have begun to be raised whether ASEAN's success at confidence-building that has underpinned the "security community" is chimerical. After all, it has been pointed out that conflicts among the member countries have not been solved. The ASEAN cohesiveness has been the result of the Cambodian conflict, the resolution of which appears closer than ever.

**Some Suggested Measures**

- Intensification of formal and informal consultations, both official and private, backed by improved mechanisms for decision-making and co-operation. This should include the institutionalization of the ASEAN Summit, which serves not only as a symbol of ASEAN unity but as a forum that promotes better understanding and empathy for each other's interests and concerns. It could serve also to discourage unilateralism, which appears to be on the rise, and is detrimental to the established norms of consensus and consultation.
- Institutionalization of procedures of conciliation to replace the existing practice of *ad hoc* self-restraint between members as the potential for greater conflicts begins to emerge.
- Greater integration of the members' armed forces. While a number of practices exist on a bilateral basis that count as military confidence-building measures, such as exchanges of visits of military personnel and students at staff colleges, exchanges of intelligence, and joint exercises, more could be done in the way of moving towards such integration.

Moreover, arms procurement by ASEAN countries is, in fact, creating tension and undermining whatever confidence may have been built over the years. Existing conflicts could worsen, as in the case of conflicts over natural resources, while new sources of conflict are emerging, including, for example, the problem of migrant labourers. For these reasons, the ASEAN process of community-building should be enhanced.

**South China Sea**

As the South China Sea is a focus of multilateral conflict with a high potential for armed confrontation, efforts should be made towards the eventual solution of the conflict. However, considering the tension that has existed especially since the Sino-Vietnamese armed clash in March 1988, confidence-building measures are required and co-operative measures must be promoted to ensure an atmosphere conducive to a negotiated settlement. Some suggested measure can be the following:

1. The freezing of all activities aimed at the occupation of additional islands in the Spratlys;
2. Renunciation of the use of force and agreement to settle disputes by peaceful means;
3. Follow-up on the Chinese proposal to set aside the issue of sovereignty, with the understanding that it is negotiable, in order to move towards negotiation on joint exploitation of resources by claimant States, bilaterally or multilaterally as the case may be;
4. Bearing in mind the strategic nature of the area as regards the safety of sea-lines of communication, the working out of co-operative measures with regard to surveillance and safety by the nations concerned, both regional and extra-regional.

## Confidence-Building Measures

As one of the largest countries in the Asia-Pacific region,

China attaches great importance to maintaining and promoting peace, security and development in this region. It is therefore interested in the related issues of regional confidence-building measures (CBMs), security and disarmament.

Significantly, in vast areas such as Asia and the Pacific, the regional confidence-building, security and disarmament issues cannot exist in isolation; on the contrary, they are closely linked to, and influenced by, what is happening globally or in other areas. If, in the global context, it is still necessary to contend with such things as the strong bullying the weak and the great harassing the small, the sovereignty of States being ignored and the arms race running wild, certainly world peace and security, including the Asian-Pacific countries and regions, will be under threat; and as a result, neither CBMs nor security and disarmament arrangements for the Asia-Pacific area can make any real progress.

In recent years, the most fundamental changes since the World War II have been occurring in the international arena, with the old world order breaking up and the new order taking definite form. Characterized by a reduction in the East-West military confrontation and by the promising prospect of the achievement of a political solution to some regional conflicts, the overall international atmosphere today has improved to some degree.

On the other hand, it is also undeniable that the world still suffers from a number of factors that constitute a threat to peace and security: the practices of hegemony and power politics have yet to be eliminated. In certain areas, political, economic or national disputes tend to deepen and worsen, leading to new tension and turbulence.

Several regional conflicts, including the conflict in the Middle East, have a long way to go and have many difficulties to overcome before achieving just and reasonable political solutions. In the field of disarmament, the momentum of the global arms race, though somewhat abating, has not come to an end.

Worse still, in some cases, it is claimed that weapons have been reduced, while in fact they have been transferred to other areas, thus causing new threats to peace and security. The proceedings of the multilateral disarmament efforts remain unsatisfactory, partly at least because of those attempts to shift the responsibility for disarmament and change the terms of certain disarmament objectives. There is a recession in the world economy and in international trade.

Consequently, the economic situation in the developing countries is becoming increasingly bleak, and, at the same time, the disparity between the developing countries and the developed world is further deepening, and the North-South polarization is worsening. Not only are these serious factors affecting world peace and security, but they also serve to confine and curb the emergence and development of regional CBMs and security and disarmament measures.

Solutions to issues in Asia and the Pacific can be found only in regard to the specific situation and characteristics of the region. This is true also in regard to the arrangements for CBMs, security and disarmament.

An idea has surfaced recently that the Conference on Security and Co-operation in Europe (CSCE) model for confidence- and security-building measures and the Negotiation on Conventional Armed Forces in Europe (CFE) model for European disarmament are panaceas that other parts of the world should prescribe for their own problems.

The progress in Europe was achieved under the particular circumstances prevailing in Europe. Experience gained in Europe can hardly apply to other regions, where the situation and conditions differ from those of Europe. Differences exist at least in the following aspects. First, for many years, Europe was dominated by two clearly delineated blocs that confronted each other both politically and militarily. No such blocs exist among the several dozens of countries in Asia and the Pacific. Secondly, the Asia-Pacific region also differs from Europe in that in this region, and, indeed, in every subregion, there are many unique conflicts and problems that are diverse in source and nature. Thirdly, while countries in Europe may be at different levels of development, they are all, on the whole, developed countries, while in Asia and the Pacific there are developed countries, developing countries and even the least developed countries. Finally, the political, social and cultural diversity among the Asian and Pacific countries is also much greater than that in Europe. In view of these major differences, there is no possibility of mechanically applying the European experience and model to this region.

- As regards the measures to be taken, CBMs should take precedence, and these should be developed into security arrangements and arrangements for disarmament at a later stage.
- In terms of geographical scope, bilateral arrangements should be given priority, followed by multilateral arrangements in small regions, which can then be gradually expanded to encompass larger areas (if needed).
- In terms of time, the institution of the CBMs and security mechanisms should be viewed as a continuous process of gradual evolution, which needs time and patience. Otherwise, we may find ourselves in a situation best described by the proverb "All haste and no speed".
- With regard to the nature of the contacts and meetings between different countries, emphasis should first be laid on scholarly discussions and low-level official contacts, which will prepare the ground for high-level meetings.

As a standard norm, different regions can only find and adopt appropriate measures to solve their problems in the light of their own specific circumstances. This is a basic principle, a principle that must be followed in exploring arrangements for CBMs, security and disarmament in Asia and the Pacific.

In line with this general approach, it is appropriate first to explore realistic and practicable CBMs. Broadly speaking, CBMs can be divided into two categories, military and non-military, which are complementary and promote each other. Given the situation in Asia and the Pacific, it would seem that the first step should be taken in the non-military field. This will prepare the ground and lay the foundation for the establishment of CBMs in the military field.

The following are applicable to the Asia-Pacific regionin connection to non-military CBMs.

1. Economic relations between countries should be established and developed on the basis of the principle of mutual benefit.
2. Political and diplomatic relations between countries should be established and developed on the basis of the principles of mutual respect for sovereignty and territorial integrity, mutual non-aggression, non-interference in the internal affairs of other countries, and peaceful coexistence.
3. An end must be put to aggression against and occupation of other countries, interference in the internal affairs of other countries and all forms of external expansion and hegemony.
4. The search for fair and reasonable political solutions to the existing problems of the regional "hot spots" must be expedited.
5. The exchange of staff and the exchange of information in the political, economic, social and cultural fields should be promoted among all countries, especially among those countries whose relations with each other, for whatever reason, are tense.

6. International disputes must be settled in a strictly peaceful manner, that is, through negotiation and consultation.
7. No country should seek to impose its social system and ideology upon other countries, much less to interfere in the internal affairs and violate the sovereignty of other countries under such pretexts.

**CBMs in Military Perspective**

- Nuclear-weapon States should undertake not to use or threaten to use nuclear weapons against non-nuclear-weapon States.
- In order to prevent the proliferation of nuclear weapons, the countries concerned may set up nuclear-weapon-free zones or zones of peace, whose status should be respected by nuclear-weapon States.
- Military bases, troops and military equipment, especially nuclear weapons, that are set up or stationed on the territory of other countries must be dismantled or withdrawn; no country in the Asia and Pacific region should send military forces overseas.
- Military equipment retired as a result of disarmament measures to other parts of the world should be destroyed. It should not be transferred to Asia and the Pacific, since such transfers will only constitute new factors of instability in this region.
- Every country should exercise self-restraint in terms of armaments and military spending and should not seek to achieve a level of armaments higher than that required for its legitimate defensive needs. Every country should also take measures to make its military strategy and the structure of its armed fores strictly defensive in nature.

It must be pointed out that the United States and the Soviet Union still maintain huge offensive armed forces in the Asia-Pacific region, including the army, the air force and blue-water fleets, posing a grave threat to other countries and exerting a negative influence on the political situation and security in this region. They should, first and foremost, take concrete measures to change this situation. In discussing the security of Asia and the Pacific, this ought to be a priority issue.

Some views and suggestions have been put forward recently by some countries regarding the security of Asia and the Pacific. These ideas are still of a rather preliminary nature and have to be developed further and clarified. We would be willing to give positive consideration to all proposals and suggestions that are conducive to the improvement of security and the maintenance of peace in the Asia-Pacific region, and to make an assessment of all the related ideas advanced by any side in the light of the basic principles mentioned above.

Generally speaking, it would not be feasible to establish an Asia-Pacific security mechanism on a large scale overnight. What should be done is rather to let things take their course and give the necessary impetus to this course as appropriate. The more urgent tasks facing the Asia-Pacific region today are, for one thing, the solution of "hot spot" issues and bilateral disputes; and for another, the strengthening of economic co-operation. The countries concerned should first advance their dialogue and consultations with one another, and take practical measures to enhance trust, reduce tension, put an end to conflicts, and strengthen security. On this basis, they could gradually establish and develop regional security mechanisms, first in small areas, and then, gradually and as circumstances require, extend them to larger regions. This would be a suitable approach in the Asia-Pacific region. Of course, issues concerning the common interest of all the countries in this region should be solved through consultations among the countries on an equal basis. If most countries tend to favour a certain form of consultation, this would certainly deserve serious and positive consideration.

# 4

# Arms Limitations in the Asia-Pacific Region: Issues and Prospect

As already mentioned, geographically, Asia-Pacific region is vast, encompassing a large number of countries which are littoral and hinterland States of the Indian Ocean and the Pacific Ocean. It is a region that has witnessed major international conflicts since the World War II.

Of course, regions and subregions cannot, be regarded as water-tight compartments. The rapid integration of the global system through political and economic interchange has been accelerated by the combined pressures of technological change, modern communications and the response to the challenge of environmental degradation. The prospects for arms limitation in one area cannot therefore be considered without taking into account the global trends set in motion by the super-Powers and developments in other regions.

Thus even the subregions of north-east Asia and south Asia are interconnected, not least by the naval presence of the superpowers in the Indian and Pacific Oceans and their naval strategies. About 50 per cent of the United States Navy was based in the Pacific, while the USSR had half its submarines there. Both have a considerable presence in the Indian Ocean. Moreover, since the Sino-Indian war of 1962 and its prelude, developments in Sino-Indian relations have had a strong influence on prospects for arms limitation in south Asia, dominated as it is by the overwhelming size of India.

Three nuclear great Powers—the USSR, the United States and China—and two potential great Powers—Japan and India—occupy dominant positions in the Asia-Pacific region as a whole. Cultural diversity and different perceptions of economic and political interest are factors that must be taken into account in their interaction, which affects the other States in the region—mostly developing countries desperately seeking conditions of peace and stability to improve the quality of life of their people and make possible the modernization of their societies.

The picture of power balance and disarmament cannot be clear without having a look at north-east Asian position.

**North-East Asia**

The north-east Asian region is characterized by the unique configuration of Powers in it and the undisputed importance of maritime Powers. The two super-Powers—the USSR and the United States—face each other across the Pacific Ocean while another great Power, China, looms large in the region together with the economic super-Power, Japan. In addition, the unresolved confrontation between North and South Korea has added tension in the region, with over 40,000 United States troops stationed in the Republic of Korea. The vast expanse of the Pacific Ocean lying between the super-Powers and the crucial importance of sea lanes for the survival of Japan's industrial powerhouse make the likelihood of naval warfare greater than in many other regions.

The area—once described by Brzezinski as the "Second Strategic Theatre"—has, since the Korean War, been regarded as a powder-keg. The 1989 *SIPRI Yearbook* notes with regard to regional military expenditures that in the mid-1980s "about 10 per cent of the world total was being spent by the countries in the Asian-Pacific region", adding that, outside of Europe, "this was the highest regional concentration of defence spending." Growth rates of defence expenditure were also noted as being high. The IISS publication *The Military Balance 1987-1988* estimates that out of a total global defence expenditure of approximately $900 billion the two super-Powers and their alliances accounted for 75 to 80 per cent, and the total Asian expenditure excluding Indochina was $65 billion or 7.2 per cent.

The dramatic economic prosperity in this subregion after the World War II has heightened its strategic importance, leading to somewhat extravagant claims of a "Pacific Century". The miracle of Japan's recovery after the Second World War and its emergence as a front-line economic Power has its own politico-strategic implications. The wider Asia-Pacific region or the Pacific Basin contains the booming newly industrializing countries (NICs), together with Australia and New Zealand, making the prosperity of the area quite broad-based.

The economic potential of the eastern Russia with its oil and gas deposits and that of China add to the economic importance of the region in global terms, especially in foreign trade, shipping and financial services. One estimate was that the subregion was containing over 20 per cent of world gross domestic product (GDP) by the year 2000, equalling that of Europe or of the United States. Trading patterns and the productivity of the area, both current and potential, convert north-east Asia into an indisputably important strategic theatre.

Due to this importance and close linkages to the two super-Powers, north-east Asia is strongly influenced by the changing relationships between those Powers. The dramatic improvement in the USSR-United States relationship in the period 1985-1990 and the bewildering velocity of political changes in Europe have had world-wide repercussions. In north-east Asia the same general improvement in international relations and prospects for disarmament and international security can be expected. At the same time, the individual roles of China and Japan and the complex relations between North and South Korea must be considered. These aspects give the subregion an internal dynamic that is unique. A detailed analysis of likely trends in arms limitation involves discussion of the approaches of the countries in the area and the interplay of their relations.

## President Gorbachev's Proposals

Relevance of the change in Soviet foreign policy brought about by Mikhail Gorbachev has not been focused on the European theatre alone. In his important Vladivostok speech of July 1986 and the Krasnoyarsk speech of September 1988 he made important proposals for the Asia-Pacific region, recognizing the United States as a Pacific Power and offering "new, fair relations in Asia and the Pacific". The proposals call for a freeze in the number of nuclear weapons in the region and reductions or a freeze in naval force deployments, especially nuclear-armed ships; a dismantling of Soviet bases in the region, provided that there is a reciprocal move by the United States; guarantees of the security of sea lanes and air communications; reduction of armed forces and conventional arms to levels of "reasonable sufficiency"; the lowering of military confrontation; and the establishment of regional negotiating machinery for confidence-building measures and arms control. The response to these proposals and actual negotiations on them have been superseded by the conclusion of the Treaty between the United States and the Soviet Union on the Elimination of Their Intermediate-Range and Shorter-Range Missiles (INF Treaty), the negotiations on a 50 per cent reduction of their strategic nuclear weapons (START), and the negotiations on conventional armed forces in Europe (CFE), which signify a preoccupation with relations between NATO and the Warsaw Treaty (WTO) having a greater priority. The proposals, however, remain on the table and will have to be addressed in any discussion of arms limitation in the Asia-Pacific region. They have been buttressed by unilateral moves such as major withdrawals of Soviet troops from Mongolia.

The self-evident priority of nuclear disarmament requires that we examine first the prospects for nuclear arms limitation in north-east Asia, where indeed the first nuclear bombs were used. Three declared nuclear Powers exist in the region. The existing INF Treaty, 70 per cent of which has been implemented today and the much-heralded and long-awaited START agreement promising a 50 per cent reduction in the strategic nuclear arsenals of the USSR and the United States will undoubtedly have their impact in the region. It has been suggested that the Soviet Union and the United States should act reciprocally to close their bases in the Pacific such as Cam Ranh Bay and Guam.

Negotiations on the United States Subic Bay naval base facility with the Philippines were expected to be tough, but the precarious position of the Aquino Government after the recent attempted coup makes any fundamental change unlikely. It is estimated that China, the USSR and the United States have nearly 3,000 nuclear warheads committed to the Pacific Ocean area. The proliferation of nuclear weapons at sea has been an alarming feature in the Pacific. Both the USSR and the United States maintain large fleets in the Pacific.

Infrastructural facilities for nuclear warfare are also located in the region by the three States. A reduction of the nuclear-weapon deployments by the USSR and the United States in this region will have to result from a global arrangement between the super-Powers. Such an arrangement should include limitations on sea-launched cruise missiles (SLCMs).

Remarkably, China's continued modernization of its nuclear arsenal—especially the 1988 nuclear weapon test believed to be of a neutron bomb, and continuing submarine-launched ballistic missile (SLBM) tests—indicates no reduction in nuclear arms despite an improving relationship with the USSR. The alleged neutron bomb test has been interpreted as a Chinese effort to develop tactical nuclear weapons, which would reflect a departure from its earlier minimal nuclear force posture, which has been confined to long-range weapon delivery systems.

The SLBM test has also caused disquiet within the region since it is seen as an indication that China is close to having nuclear-powered ballistic missile submarines with operational capability. A related development was the Chinese sale of intermediate-range ballistic missiles to Saudi Arabia, although these were modified to carry conventional warheads. The implication is that China is phasing out this category of missiles and developing a new generation of missiles and that it is also a source of ballistic missile proliferation, and this has created great concern. Despite these developments, the political crisis caused by the events in Tiananmen Square in June 1989 and the severe austerity programme launched by the Chinese leadership are bound to affect China's nuclear arms development programme.

Despite the fact that both the Republic of Korea and the Democratic People's Republic of Korea have signed the Treaty on the Non-Proliferation of Nuclear Weapons, rumours have persisted about clandestine nuclear-weapon programmes. Full access by the International Atomic Energy Agency (IAEA) to nuclear power plants in the Korean peninsula would enhance confidence in the region.

## Chemical Weapons

The danger from chemical weapons does not appear to be a major problem in north-east Asia, and with moves in the Conference on Disarmament to achieve the speedy conclusion of a comprehensive chemical weapons ban instrument, one can safely conclude that the prospect of the development and use of chemical weapons in north-east Asia is unlikely. There have, however, been allegations traded between the two Koreas regarding the stockpiling of chemical weapons. China's sale of missiles outside the region has also led to fears that the purchasers may equip such missiles to carry chemical weapons. Within the larger Asia-Pacific region, Australia has proposed creating a chemical-weapon-free zone in the Pacific.

### Conventional Weapons

With regard to conventional weapons, economic pressures have prompted Soviet initiatives for arms limitation and caused an actual decline in China's military expenditure. In China, political changes led to important defence reductions linked to new military strategies. China's military forces were cut by 1 million troops, and large defence industries were converted to serve civilian needs. The pragmatic trends in China's foreign policy appeared to suffer a set-back following the June 1989 crisis and the sharp international reaction to it. However, China's acceptance of a United Nations role in the resolution of the Cambodian problem, Li Peng's visit to Moscow and other attempts by China to resume its international responsibilities augur well. The pattern of reduced defence spending is likely to continue, largely because of economic pressures and the restructuring that is going on within China. According to official statistics, the share of the defence budget in the total budget was halved, to around 8 per cent, in 1988.

In Japan, concerns have been expressed regarding the breach of the self-imposed ceiling of 1 per cent of GNP for defence expenditure. The last budget showed a growth of 5.2 per cent in defence expenditure and this upward trend is expected to continue. Japan has emerged as one of the top six military spenders in the world. It has, however, been argued that the strengthening of the yen *vis-a-vis* the United States dollar has inflated Japanese defence spending. While in real terms defence expenditure has increased and an expansion of military capability has occurred, Japan remains defence-oriented in terms of article 9 of its Constitution and without a long-range attack capability. Its arms production remains low. Moreover, United States pressures for burden-sharing have contributed to Japan's increased allocations for defence. In the period 1984-1988 Japan was the fourth largest importer of arms, most of which came from the United States.

Defence expenditures by North and South Korea remain high. Economic constraints and policy shifts at the top may lead to changes in North Korea, especially if there is an acceleration of the current North-South conciliatory moves. North Korea was the eighth largest importer of arms in the period 1984-1988. Its possession of Scud missile technology and of the fourth largest air force in the world is significant. South Korea too has a missile capability. So does Taiwan.

The Soviet-United States negotiations on arms reductions and limitations have a greater potential to improve prospects for arms limitation in north-east Asia than in south Asia. It should at the minimum decrease United States-USSR arms supplies, which in the period 1971-1985 accounted for 80 per cent of the total volume. The progress of USSR-China *rapprochement* is also important for developments in north-east Asia and its security environment. Tensions in the Korean peninsula remain, however, and have shown themselves to be governed more by indigenous factors than by great-Power relations in the area—although the problem has in the past been exacerbated by super-Power rivalry. The Japan-United States security nexus is also an important factor in the subregion. An improvement in Russia-United States relations alone will not be sufficient to allay Japanese apprehensions of the USSR, and progress in resolving disputes between the USSR and Japan is necessary.

Now a look at the strategic and defence situation at South Asia.

**South Asia**

In the south Asian subregion we are confronted by the fact of India's overwhelming size and power. Relations between India and its neighbours, especially Pakistan, are crucial to the stability of the area. The Indian Ocean, with the prospect of naval competition within it, is another important factor.

**Nuclear Weapons**

The peaceful nuclear explosion carried out by India in 1974, together with its refusal to sign the non-proliferation Treaty, has led to persistent rumours of India's nuclear-weapon capability. Policies pursued since the time of Zulfiquar Ali Bhutto in Pakistan, evidence of clandestine acquisition of technology and *materiel,* and the existence of the unsafeguarded Kahuta enrichment plant have also led to suspicions that Pakistan—which is also outside the NPT regime—is engaged in a clandestine nuclear-weapon programme. At any rate, both countries are commonly referred to as nuclear "threshold" States with a nuclear-weapon capability. While both have officially proclaimed that their nuclear programmes are for peaceful purposes, they have also asserted that they could build the bomb if they so wished. The perception of a nuclear arms race between India and Pakistan, even if it is not based on fact, has a destabilizing influence.

Since the partition in 1947 the two countries have been at war on three occasions. Despite the Simla Accords of 1972, tensions have waxed and waned. Domestic unrest in India, specifically in the Punjab and in Jammu and Kashmir, has been blamed on Pakistan, and mutual suspicions have lingered. The emergence of a democratically elected government in Pakistan led by Benazir Bhutto presented an opportunity for change. Her statement rejecting a nuclear-weapon option for Pakistan and the agreement reached with India on 31 December 1988 to exchange information on nuclear plants and not to attack each other's nuclear installations have opened a new chapter. By now (2010AD) India has developed nuclear capability of high order. Its missile project and space technology is one of the best in world. Though an old partner of USSR (now Russia) in defence matters, now in changed new world order the USA is gradually aheading towards mutual partnership in strategic matters with India.

Pakistan on the other hand is an old accomplice of USA, receiving huge funds in the name of development and fighting terrorism (though Pakistan itself is the perpetrator of terrorism in the region). Pakistan has also developed nuclear warheads Due to political instability and internal conflicts in the country a danger of reaching those warheads in the hands of terrorists and Islamic fundamentalists in looming before the world community. Simultaneously,, Pakistan's missile programme in connivance with China and Korea is a major threat to world peace.

Sino-Indian relations could not yet become cordial. Though in the field of trade there has been some progress, China is a danger to India in strategic matters. Recently infiltration of Chinese troops in Indian border, its presence in Pak-occupied Kashmir and other such incidents give support to this fear. Bangladesh and Nepal have also shown hostile attitude towards India of late. In Sri Lanka, though internal civil war is calmed, Pakistan is developing strategic relations with her, which may also cause suspicion for peace in the Indian Ocean region.

**Chemical Weapons**

The south Asian subregion is not known to have any stocks of chemical weapons, and although allegations of the use of such weapons in Afghanistan have been made, these were directed against the USSR. South Asian States have co-operated in the international quest for a comprehensive ban on chemical weapons.

## Conventional Weapons

Remarkably, there is no denying the fact that India's conventional armed forces are widely regarded as being in excess of its subregional needs even if Pakistan is regarded as a threat. India's smaller neighbours can only aspire to be minor irritants. Thus India's armed might has an extra-subregional rationale, ostensibly for defence against an extra-subregional threat. Its purchases for the period 1984-1988 placed India as the second largest procurer of conventional weapons in the world—next only to Iraq, which was involved in a war with Iran at the time. India's blue-water naval capability was enhanced significantly with the lease of nuclear-powered attack submarines from the USSR. Its domestic arms production sector has grown and India has become an arms exporter.

India's missile programme has also led to concern, both within and outside south Asia. It has been known that India had a programme for developing space launch vehicles (SLVs), which was described as being for civilian purposes. In addition, a military missile programme has been initiated, and in February 1988 a ballistic missile (known as the Prithvi) with a range of 250 km and a pay load of about 1000 kg was successfully tested. A larger ballistic missile (the Agni), officially described as being for research purposes and with a longer range of 2400 km, was successfully tested on 22 May 1989. The combination of India's acquisition of nuclear-powered submarines and the development of missiles with longer ranges than necessary for purely defensive requirements represents a qualitative escalation in the militarization of south Asia.

Pakistan's military expenditure received a major boost following the intervention of the USSR in Afghanistan and the conversion of the country as a base for Afghan *muja-heddin* resistance to the pro-Soviet Government installed in Kabul. SIPRI'S tentative figures place Pakistan's military expenditure at between 6.6 and 6.9 per cent of GDP during the period 1981-1986 (India's was between 3 and 3.7 per cent). In April 1988 Pakistan announced the testing of two types of ballistic missiles. On 5 February 1989 a further test, of a surface-to-surface long-range missile, was announced. Pakistan also has a civilian rocket research programme and a space-launch vehicle programme. With Pakistan's nuclear-weapon capability having been widely proven, attention has been focused on the possible delivery of such weapons by long-range aircraft. With the withdrawal of Soviet troops from Afghanistan and negotiations with a view to arriving at a permanent settlement of the Afghan problem the rationale for these forms of military expenditure by Pakistan has diminished. However, until the various issues are negotiated, tensions will remain between India and Pakistan. Various terrorists group like Al-Qaeda, Lashkare-Toiba and Taliban etc. supported and guided by ISI of Pakistan are operative in the region.

Military expenditure in other countries of south Asia is not so significant as to pose a threat to the stability of their neighbours. In Sri Lanka, while the internal conflicts caused by Tamil militant groups and the People's Liberation Front continue at horrendously brutal levels, actual defence expenditure has begun to decline. The Sri Lanka phenomenon and the Sikh agitation in India focus on the problem of arms acquisition by sub-national groups and the need for curbs on the arms trade. The abortive Maldivian coup of 1988, which employed mercenaries, highlighted the special security needs of small States and led to the adoption, at the forty-fourth session of the General Assembly, of a resolution, sponsored by Maldives, on the use of mercenaries.

## The Indian Ocean as a Zone of Peace

India Ocean once a peaceful area was infested with so called super power and western naval vessels, establishing naval bases in the region. Hence a disturbed zone. Despite cessation of cold war, Indian Ocean is still not bed of naval activities.

The implementation of the 1971 United Nations Declaration of the Indian Ocean as a Zone of Peace would be a key factor in achieving arms limitation in South Asia. Despite favourable developments in the relationship between the super-Powers, the withdrawal of Soviet forces from Afghanistan and the progress achieved in other regional conflicts, the convening of the Conference to convert the Indian Ocean into a zone of peace remains a controversial issue. At its most recent meeting, the three Western nuclear weapon Powers announced their decision to withdraw from the *Ad Hoc* Committee on the Indian Ocean, while all but two of the remaining Western States decided not to participate in the committee's work.

This has added further complications to the functioning of the *Ad Hoc* Committee and the negotiations for the convening of the Conference. Within the *Ad Hoc* Committee on the Indian Ocean a host of proposals have been made for confidence-building measures on land and at sea. At the Meeting of the Littoral and Hinterland States of the Indian Ocean held in 1979 a set of principles was adopted forming a code of conduct. Adherence to this code would undoubtedly encourage arms limitation in the area, and an initiative could be taken by Indian Ocean States outside the *Ad Hoc* Committee. The presence in the *Ad Hoc* Committee of the permanent members of the Security Council, the major maritime users of the Indian Ocean and other Member States has made the task of achieving consensus a difficult one. A date for the Colombo Conference with universal participation is the first issue on which there has to be a consensus before the Indian Ocean can be converted into a zone of peace binding the countries both within and outside the region to a code ensuring regional peace and security and facilitating arms reduction both on land and at sea.

—

"There is a ubiquitous desire to turn over a new leaf, to try innovative approaches for the solution of old problems. In diverse regions, there is weariness with wars and there is recognition of their futility. Nor do the postures of hostile competition have the appeal to public opinion that they unfortunately exerted not too long ago. Instead, it is the combat against the causes of conflict, the struggle against economic inequities and social evils and the degradation of the environment that must evoke all the courage and determination of battle."

—*Perez de Cuellar (1989)*

## Naval Arms

Both the Pacific Ocean and the Indian Ocean are characterized by a high level of military activity; hence the subject of curbing the naval arms race must be addressed. While the navies of the super-Powers enjoy dominant positions, there is also concern about the growing naval strength of States in the Asia-Pacific region. The need to include naval arms control in the disarmament negotiations between the United States and the USSR is urgent. The risk of incidents at sea leading to war is grave. Economic constraints have already acted in the United States to reduce the naval budget, and this factor alone may result in naval arms limitation. Arguments that an asymmetry exists between the two superpowers, with the United States perceiving itself as a maritime island nation having a genuine need to protect its sea links for national security reasons, have been advanced to justify its global naval presence and to oppose moves towards naval arms control.

Proposals by the USSR such as those made in President Gorbachev's Vladivostok and Krasnoyarsk statements in pursuit of naval arms control have thus met with a negative response. However, the inclusion of SLBM launches in the 1988 Ballistic Missile Launch Notification Agreement and the application to the naval area of the 1989 Prevention of Dangerous Military Activities Agreement indicate that small steps are possible as confidence-building measures. Even if actual reductions of naval forces do not take place, the adoption of a number of limited measures, such as notification of naval exercises, negotiation of a multilateral incidents-at-sea regime, and exchanges of information, appear possible. The measures are global in scope but should be of major effect in reducing tensions, caused by the naval arms race, in the Indian and Pacific Oceans.

Francis Fukuyama has discerned in the tumultuous events of the recent past a triumph of liberal democracy over Marxism-Leninism, which he has perhaps presumptuously labelled "the end of history", deriving the notion from the Marxist view of history as a dialectical process and the Hegelian view that history is motivated by overcoming contradictions between thesis and antithesis. Others have demurred over this hyperbole and have referred to an acceleration of history with "imperial overstretch" affecting both the United States and the USSR. Both notions reflect essentially a Eurocentric view, the applicability of which to the Asia-Pacific region is more apparent than real.

The non-aligned countries in the Asia-Pacific region have long and consistently stood for an independent approach to international relations outside the contradiction between the two alliances of the post-World War II bipolar world, portrayed at the time in Manichaean terms. Safeguarding their national independence from all forms of domination and intervention, these nations have for decades been pledged to the principles of peace, disarmament and the democratization of international relations, and to multilateral co-operation, especially through the United Nations. The inception of the Movement of Non-aligned Countries can in fact be traced to the Bandung Conference of 1955 in the Asia-Pacific region. Fukuyama himself in a subsequent article looks ahead to "a world where economic concerns are dominant, where no ideological grounds exist for major conflict between nations, and where, consequently, the use of military force becomes less legitimate". He adds:

> "Consumers do not always want what can be measured in GNP. They also demand things like clean air and a safe environment for their children, and it is this broader set of goals that will shape the political agendas, both domestic and international, of the post-historical world."

The emergence of the NICs in the Asia-Pacific region, the post-1979 economic reforms in China, and the achievement of self-sufficiency in cereals in India are examples of the region's economic advances in comparison to other areas. This demonstrated pragmatic concern with basic economic development issues diminishes the danger of military confrontation and increases the prospects for arms limitation. National rivalries will of course continue and ethnic nationalism will persist in acquiring militant forms. A decrease, if not the total elimination, of the great-Power presence in the region is crucial and would reduce tensions and create conditions of peace and security. That has yet to take place as a logical sequel to improving East-West relations.

Trade wars are more likely being fought in the forums of the General Agreement on Tariffs and Trade (GATT) and the United Nations Conference on Trade and Development (UNCTAD) than by arms. As the components of power change slowly but surely from the politico-military to the economic we are witnessing a multipolar world of a different kind. No doubt, large-scale wars between nations have become less likely. That in itself will be a force for demilitarization but it can come in the Asia-Pacific region only with the great Powers taking the lead.

## Evolving a Security Consensus

The pattern of regional co-operation for peace and development is unique for each region. No model can be entirely replicated elsewhere. However, lessons can be learned from the successes and failures of others. The experience of Helsinki and Stockholm must therefore be examined objectively. With so much cultural diversity and other disparities amongst the countries of the region, we are a long way from talking of a common Asia-Pacific home. While the danger of large-scale conflict may have been averted with the improved international atmosphere, the pressures for disarmament in the Asia-Pacific region are still not as strong as they should be.

On 16 January 1990, a three-week colloquium began in Vienna among the chiefs of staff of European countries on military doctrines. It is perhaps time for a similar dialogue among the nations of the Asia-Pacific region as a first step towards an understanding of one another's legitimate interests and aspirations. It is only after a regional consensus is reached, accommodating the national interests of all, that genuine arms limitation and disarmament measures can be implemented. Regional security leading to disarmament is best and more durably achieved through consensus arrangements than through the emergence of regional Powers as gendarmes. Some of the regional organizations in the Asia-Pacific region—ASEAN, the South Asian Association for Regional Co-operation and the South Pacific Forum—have the potential of developing such a consensus following further advances towards their present goals for economic co-operation.

A further prospect for arms limitations and disarmament in the Asia-Pacific region lies in the concept of "non-offensive defence", also known as "non-provocative defence" and" alternative defence". Developed in the European context, the conceptual objective is to achieve conventional stability by maximizing the defensive orientation of forces, thus reducing the danger of surprise attack and achieving security at lower overall levels of armaments. It is claimed that it is possible to achieve structural incapacity to attack, thereby reducing threat perceptions and enhancing confidence. At a recent symposium, UNIDIR invited a group of scholars and diplomats to explore the applicability of "non-offensive defence" to other regions as a preliminary attempt to broaden the discussion of this concept. While the primacy of political factors cannot be denied, the influence of military doctrines that assure equal national security is also important, and further exploration of new concepts is urgent.

## CONFIDENCE- AND SECURITY-BUILDING MEASURES (CSBM) AND MILITARY SECURITY

In the present chapter, we will try to examines a number of problems which the negotiation and implementation of confidence-building measure (CBM) regimes may pose for military planners. It is written in the conviction that CBMs can play a vitally important role in enhancing military security outside the European framework. But it stresses that for CBM regimes to be negotiated and implemented effectively, security planners need to be forewarned about the problems which may arise in the process.

According to a "confidence-building measure" is, James Macintosh a concept notable for the imprecision of various attempts to define it. There is little consensus about what may be included under the general rubric of confidence-building measures or how they are to be distinguished from other arms control measures. There is also confusion over the critically important question of what CBMs are intended to achieve—and whose confidence is supposed to be built by CBM regimes.

Are CBMs intended to engender confidence on one side about the benign intentions of the other? Or vice versa? Or both? And even if the nature and goals of CBMs can be agreed upon, this still leaves unresolved the almost wholly unresearched issue of what are the psychological mechanisms by which confidence may be built.

### Relevance of CBMs to Coping with Unprovoked Aggression

It is pertinent to note that it is probably true to say that much of the support for CBMs within the Western arms control community has been predicated on the assumption that the major risk of armed conflict between the rival alliances arose, not from unprovoked aggression, but from a crisis escalating out of control and propelling adversaries into an unintended confrontation. CBMs, in other words, were seen as most relevant to the goal of minimizing the dangers of inadvertent war.

But if premeditated and unprovoked aggression, rather than crisis instability, is assumed to constitute the central security problem, the strategic utility of CBMs may be questioned. Attempts by our side to reassure an adversary bent on aggression about our intentions will be, at best, futile and at worst amount to appeasement. The confidence which the British believed had been built at Munich between Neville Chamberlain and Adolf Hitler turned out to be a sad delusion.

Jonathan Alford has defined CBMs as "measures that tend to make military intentions obvious." CBMs thus defined are clearly highly relevant to military security. Indeed the Alford definition is synonymous with good intelligence and good intelligence would be a great value to any nation facing an adversary bent on aggression. In third world States which lack the sophisticated surveillance and intelligence capabilities of the super-Powers, information CBMs, such as those advocated by Shultz and Alford, may be a particularly useful hedge against surprise attack.

Does this mean that CBMs are of no use in the face of potentially aggressive adversaries? Not necessarily. At the Conference on Confidence- and Security-building Measures and Disarmament in Europe (CDE) in Stockholm, the then United States Secretary of State, George Shultz, defined the United States objective at the talks as the achievement of a CBM regime which would "reduce the danger of surprise attack, miscalculation, or misunderstanding".

What then does it mean to say that measures designed to clarify military intentions and contribute to decreasing the risk of surprise attack are confidence-building measures? The short answer is that while they may not build mutual confidence, they may well create confidence on our side about our ability to detect aggressive preparations by adversaries early enough to make an appropriate defensive response. From a purely military point of view this is highly desirable.

The strong emphasis on the military utility of CBMs which was stressed by the NATO side at the Stockholm negotiations is partly responsible for the increasing adoption of the term "confidence- and *security-building,* measures" (CSBMs).

It is of course true that a State bent on aggression might well refuse to negotiate a CBM regime which minimized the chances of its aggression succeeding. But the refusal to negotiate should in itself have a useful cautionary effect.

In accepting above argument, it would seem to follow that the most limited CSBMs are those which increase a nation's own confidence in its abilities to detect an adversary's preparations for acts of aggression. More extensive CSBMs (i.e. those where confidence may be increased on both sides) are relevant where neither side in fact harbours aggressive intentions against the other, but where the relationship between the two is nevertheless characterized by a considerable degree of suspicion and hostility. Here the confidence-building process—a process which seeks to reduce hostility and fear—should be mutual.

Now some pertinent issues.

**Threat Surprise Attack**

A central North Atlantic Treaty Organization (NATO) objective at the Stockholm Conference was to negotiate CSBMs which would reduce the risk of surprise attack.

NATO's concern was understandable. Western analysts believed that Soviet strategy for the Central Front in Europe sought to exploit the advantage of surprise in blitzkrieg-type offensive thrusts against NATO forces. CSBMs which made Moscow's strategic task more difficult were clearly in NATO's interest. But herein lay a problem. In so far as surprise attack is seen by one side (or indeed both) as having clear military utility when war is perceived to be inevitable, what security interest does the side contemplating a surprise attack have in negotiating CSBMs designed to undercut this tactic?

Anti-surprise-attack CSBMs would certainly have had no appeal for Israel in June 1967. Israel's extraordinary success in the Six-Day War owed an enormous amount to the pre-emptive surprise attack launched by the Israeli Defence Force which destroyed many of the combat aircraft of Syria and Egypt on the ground. Similarly, the strong emphasis in the United States Navy's maritime strategy on the need for initiative and surprise may be a determinate factor in the Navy's strong resistance to naval CSBMs which might reduce the element of surprise.

The problem of surprise attack is related to the more general problems raised by offensive strategies and force structures which are addressed in the conclusion.

### CSBMs and Deterrence

A burning question is, can CSBMs undermine deterrence and in so doing increase the risk of aggression? The reasons the United States Navy advances for its opposition to a range of CSBM constraint measures illustrate how particular security concerns may lead to the rejection of CSBMs. The Navy's argument runs roughly as follows: Constraints on exercises (as proposed by the Soviets on a number of occasions) will prevent the Navy from practising its strategy effectively. In so far as this is true the Navy's war-fighting capability will decline, which will in turn undermine deterrence and thus increase the risk of aggression. CSBMs, in other words, may actually increase the risk of war. When it is pointed out that the CSBM constraints apply to both sides, the Navy is quick to respond that its activities will be affected far more than those of the Soviet side, since United States ships are forward deployed, while the Soviet Navy is more defensively oriented and its operating tempo has slowed considerably over the past years.

**False Confidence**

Pressures to achieve negotiated arms control agreements are likely to be most intense when there is widespread public enthusiasm for such agreements, when a perceived reluctance to reach an agreement could be politically costly to the Government conducting the negotiations, and when the adversary is making apparently reasonable proposals. Under such circumstances agreements may be made for essentially domestic political reasons, which could have adverse long-term security consequences. Agreements which create the illusion of progress where there is no substance may have a dangerously lulling effect on public consciousness—this may be a particular problem with CSBM regimes. False confidence may lead to a dangerous decline in vigilance. While it is true that CSBMs are intended, among other things, to reduce the risks of surprise attack, they will only succeed in doing this if the warnings that are generated are heeded.

If Governments and publics have been lulled into a sense of false confidence, there is a strong possibility that these warnings will be ignored or misinterpreted. Quite apart from military objections to CSBMs in principle, there are a range of problems which may arise in the negotiating process itself.

The ways in which adversaries perceive security may be very different and the differences may in themselves generate suspicion during the negotiating process. In the

Stockholm negotiations, for example, the Russians initially placed great emphasis on "declaratory" or "political" CSBMs. According to Barry Blechman such CSBMs, could:

> "... signal the desire of those States party to the agreement to adopt a co-operative posture in regional affairs. This type of declaration could be a necessary precedent to further arms control negotiations. It could be used to clear the air of past grievances and to signal the beginning of new relationships. A further and very important purpose would be to demonstrate the political commitment of the signatory States to sustain the policies required to bring about stabilization in the region".

Surprisingly, the United States has traditionally rejected the Soviet emphasis on such political/legal CBMs, arguing that they are largely inspired by propagandistic motives. Soviet statements of peaceful intent were disbelieved because of the very American suspicions that they were ostensibly intended to dispel.

On the other hand, Soviet Union, had tended to argue that the gravest risks of war were to be found in political relationships, and their negotiating style had reflected these concerns. From the Soviet perspective, the United States approach was unhelpful, since, in focusing on narrow military/technical CSBMs, it dealt with the symptoms of the super-Power conflict and ignored its fundamental causes. They argued that crisis-avoidance is a more prudent security goal than crisis-stability. They further suggest that crisis-avoidance is best approached via political CSBMs rather than the military/technical CSBMs favoured by NATO.

Thus Moscow has repeatedly stressed the importance of declaratory agreements such as the 1972 basic principles Agreement, stressing the need to avoid situations likely to lead to increased tensions, and the 1973 Agreement on the Prevention of Nuclear War.

The then Soviets have argued that the military/technical

CSBMs which NATO promoted were largely irrelevant to the task of preventing crises from arising in the first place. NATO, on the other hand, has wanted "... deeds, not words or sweeping pledges, to be the basis of confidence- and security-building efforts in Europe."

It is remarkable that on the Korean peninsula quite different security mindsets have also prevented progress towards creating even the most modest CSBM regime. For the Democratic People's Republic of Korea (North Korea), the central security goal is reunification of the two Koreas and the central negotiating task is to construct a blueprint for reaching that goal. The Republic of Korea (South Korea) agrees that reunification is an ultimate goal but believes that a minimal degree of trust must be created between the two sides before negotiations on reunification—or the form that it will take—can commence.

Modest CSBMs are seen as a means towards the latter end. However, scholars from the North have argued that the CSBMs advocated by the South would have the effect of reinforcing the *status quo* of a divided Korea and would thus be antithetical to the eventual goal of reunification. The Republic of Korea sees the Democratic People's Republic of Korea's reluctance to countenance even the most modest CSBMs as evidence of Pyongyang's bad faith.

Discussions on military doctrine, with the various parties seeking an empathetic understanding of each other's security perspective, could be particularly helpful in this respect. In other conflict situations adversaries may have quite different but equally incompatible security mindsets which may create barriers to progress. But such problems will be alleviated if they are recognized and addressed at the outset.

**Asymmetrical Impact of CSBMs**

Another major difficulty which may be encountered in negotiating CSBMs derives from the fact that the measures proposed often impact very differently on the parties which are subject to them. The Stockholm Conference negotiating record again provides a number of usefully cautionary examples.

In this connection it is noteworthy that on January 1984, NATO presented six measures for negotiation at the Stockholm Conference. These measures included exchanges of military data, advance notification of military activities, observation of military activities, verification of military activities and enhanced communication procedures. Richard Damek has noted that in this list of CSBMs, "the quest for information predominates, especially information provided by the other side." The Soviets saw this stress on information-gathering as little more than legalized espionage—and complained that NATO's proposals meant that the United States would be able to spy on much of the USSR, while United States territory was not subject to transparency inspections by the East.

Moscow's concern arose because, even though transparency CSBMs might be applied equally to all sides, they would in practice provide the West with more information about the closed and traditionally secretive East than vice versa. Moscow could glean detailed information on military developments in the United States from such public domain sources as Congressional Hearings, the National Technical Information Service, and even *The New York Times.* There were no comparable sources of public information in the Soviet public domain accessible to the United States and its allies. The key point here is that asymmetry in existing access to information meant that transparency CSBMs, when implemented, would confer a disproportionate advantage on one side.

Remarkably, among the constraint CSBMs proposed by the East at the Stockholm negotiations were certain prohibitions on the size of exercises. The standard United States response to all constraint proposals was that "it was difficult to conceive of measures that did not impact disproportionately on NATO."

Indeed the Soviet proposal for a ceiling of 40,000 troops on manoeuvres would have had the effect of constraining NATO far more than the Warsaw Treaty States, which traditionally exercised with smaller troop numbers than NATO. A number of the USSR's naval arms control proposals would also impact far more on the forward-deployed United States Navy than on the more defensively deployed Soviet Navy—this has been one of the reasons advanced by the United States Navy for its persistent rejection of proposals for naval arms control.

The fact that some constraint measures may impact more on one side than another is, however, not a good reason for rejecting constraint measures *per se.* It does suggest that if negotiations are being conducted in good faith (they may be engaged in for propagandistic reasons), then great care should be taken to try to avoid advocacy of particular CSBMs which, even though they might be applied symmetrically, would impact asymmetrically—i.e., would disadvantage one side more than the other.

Negotiating teams are comprised of individuals who very frequently represent different bureaucratic interests as well as their own individual views as to what the real goals of the negotiation process should be. Thus for every committed arms controller on the team, there may be one or more others who see the negotiation process as simply another arena in which the adversarial struggle should be played out. From the latter perspective, the name of the game is to gain a military or political advantage over the other side, not the achievement of greater common security. As Stephen Larrabee and Alien Lynch observed of the Stockholm process:

> "Since each side tends to put forward those CBMs that constrain the behaviour of the other, while

> resisting those that would inhibit its own, progress in negotiating CBMs has been slow."

## The Negotiation Process

Even where there is a genuine will to achieve an agreement, its achievement may be frustrated by failures in the negotiation process. It is somewhat ironic that, while arms control negotiating teams usually include military, legal, technical, political and arms control experts, they almost never include experts in the process of negotiation *per se*. It is sometimes the case that negotiations fail because there is simply no basis for a satisfactory resolution of the issues being addressed. But at other times they fail not because the dispute was inherently insoluble, but because of avoidable failures in the negotiation process itself. The case for negotiating teams to include experts in the process of negotiation—or at least for providing negotiators with training in negotiating skills—would appear to be compelling. This is particularly true with respect to CSBMs, where the issues being discussed may well be more sensitive than is the case with force-reduction negotiations. Some interesting work in this area has already been undertaken by Roger Fisher and William Ury of the Harvard Negotiation Project.

Where negotiations reach an impasse there may be a case for mediation or other forms of intervention by third parties in whom both sides have confidence. For example, North and South Korean arms control experts have each noted the similarity of the other's proposals to create a genuine demilitarized zone along the border between their two countries.

## How to Implement?

In fact, even when CSBM agreements have been successfully negotiated, their practical implementation may be a process which actually undermines confidence and is fraught with frustration. Colonel Jim E. Hinds, a retired United States army officer who had been involved in observing a number of Soviet military activities, clearly found the experience a thoroughly negative one.

Commenting on his experiences as an observer under the terms of the 1975 Helsinki Final Act, Hinds notes:

> "Observers were only permitted to witness demonstrations, not manoeuvres. They were not permitted to provide their own equipment, not permitted freedom of movement, but were transported by Soviet hosts, and were given no opportunities freely to interview Soviet officers or soldiers."

Most of the problems which were associated with the Helsinki CBMs have been overcome in the Stockholm regime, but the difficulties with the Helsinki regime implementation offer a useful warning of possible implementation problems for States contemplating creating CSBM regimes in non-European theatres.

It should also be recognized that the "arms control paradox", namely, that arms control is hardest to negotiate when most needed and easiest to negotiate when least needed, applies with particular force to CSBMs. There will undoubtedly be times when levels of hostility and suspicion between adversaries are simply too high for CSBM negotiations to have any chance of succeeding. In such circumstances it is better to avoid negotiations at the official level completely. But even where official bilateral negotiations are impossible, so-called "track II diplomacy" involving unofficial meetings, possibly between scholars and former officials, may fulfil a useful role. Furthermore, detailed consideration of possible CSBM regimes within the security communities on each side may facilitate negotiations when hostility declines.

Under certain circumstances it is possible to imagine examples where this might be true—though the history of CSBM negotiations suggests that the parties to them rarely compromise what they perceive as their essential security interests. But what is critical to stress here is that any approach to security has drawbacks. The fact that CSBM regimes under certain circumstances may pose certain risks is, in itself, no argument against seeking to achieve them. The critical question is whether, in creating a CSBM regime, the balance of risk is, or is not, outweighed by the balance of advantage.

This is particularly pertinent when looking at the alternatives advocated by critics of CSBMs—alternatives which stress deterrence rather than reassurance, national security rather than common security, and pre-emption rather than withholding. Such alternatives are most frequently associated with offence-dominant force structures and strategies. The argument for offensively-oriented strategies and force postures is that these enhance deterrence and offer a more efficacious mode of war-fighting if deterrence nevertheless fails. Both of these assumptions are open to question. But whatever their claimed advantages in the realm of war-fighting, there is no doubt that offensive strategies undermine policies of both crisis-avoidance and crisis-control.

Because offensive forces can be used for aggression as well as in response to aggression, their very existence is bound to generate suspicion in the minds of prudent defence planners on the other side. Offensive force postures do not, of course, cause conflicts, but they may well exacerbate them, while at the same time providing rationales for arms races. Because they place considerable emphasis on preemption and on escalation once the threshold to war has been crossed, offensive strategies are also inimical to crisis-stability.

In seeking to maximize deterrence against unprovoked aggression, they may unwittingly increase the risk of inadvertent war. Offensive strategies, in other words, are quite antithetical to confidence-building.

In considering whether or not the CSBM/defensive strategy path to security may be as useful for regions outside Europe as it clearly has been for those within, it will be necessary to bear in mind not only the particular problems which negotiating and implementing the CSBMs will involve, but also the broader question of what is the most probable cause of war in the region in question.

Defensive strategies are designed to eliminate incentives for pre-emption in crises and escalation in war by abjuring the capability seriously to threaten an adversary, while retaining the capability for effective defence. Most constraint CSBMs may be seen as contributions to the creation of defensive force postures. Indeed, defensive force postures and strategies may in one sense be seen as the ultimate form of constraint CSBMs. In Europe, however, negotiations to reduce capabilities for large-scale offensive operations are being conducted at a separate venue (the Negotiation on Conventional Armed Forces in Europe (CFE)) from the ongoing talks on CSBMs in Vienna.

## Environment and Parameters for Asia-Pacific CSBMs

When considering CSBMs and a CSCE-type of arrangement in Asia and the Pacific, we are talking about a very vast area, stretching from the Middle East or western Asia and the Persian Gulf to East Asia and the Pacific, including Australia and New Zealand and the islands of the South Pacific Ocean. Europe, by comparison, is rather small—and we have to be very clear about the sheer expanse of the area we are talking about.

In fact, the geographical, historical, political, cultural and social heterogeneity of the area has to be taken into account. There is, of course, heterogeneity in Europe, but there is much more homogeneity than exists in Asia. Indeed, in Asia and the Pacific there is no common identity or consciousness except, in practical terms, in a very basic and minimal sense. Instead, the best we can argue for in Asia and the Pacific is subregional consciousness or identity. For the many countries in this region which emerged from colonialism only after the Second World War, not only is there very little sense of regionalism—and any that exists is very nascent and embryonic—but there is more nationalism than anything else. There is nothing comparable to the ongoing process of European regional integration in Asia and the Pacific in any pan-Asian sense.

It is pertinent to note that there arrangements of course have an impact on prospects for CSBMs in the area and its respective subregions and for any CSCE-type of organization in the area. There are no shared historical or security perceptions for the area as a whole, and this would rather limit any prospect for any application of CSCE concepts across the whole region. The best one could hope for, for the near term and foreseeable future, if CSCE-type regimes are wanted in the area, would be subregional schemes. Several other factors indicate the same limitation, and will be addressed later.

One should also consider the multiplicity of balances of power or separate theatres that the region contains in contrast to the very clear bipolar power configuration of post-war Europe, at least until recently. In Asia, there is, or was, the super-Power balance and even today it exists in the North-East Asian subregion. It was superimposed, however, upon a number of local balances of power—in the Middle East, in South Asia, in South-East Asia, in the South Pacific and even in North-East Asia. So we have had overlapping, multiple conglomerations of power balances in the region, unlike in Europe. This factor will of course heavily influence regimes of the CSCE type throughout the area.

Obviously, there are great asymmetries of power across this vast region, which further complicate CSBM and arms reduction efforts, whether these are on a region-wide, subregional or even bilateral basis. These asymmetries are of two types: between nations as a whole, and between the different characteristics of their military power, including whether it is land-based, air-based or naval, and whether it is conventional or nuclear. There are, of course, the big-Powers, the United States and the Russia, which stand apart, at least in the nuclear sense. Then there are the major Powers of the region, China, Japan and India. Thirdly, there are what could be called middle Powers: Indonesia, the Koreas, Pakistan and Viet Nam. Finally, there are the lesser Powers, some of the weakest and smallest in the world. Thus some of the most powerful and some of the weakest countries in the world are represented in Asia and the Pacific. In view of these asymmetries of power, there is little room for reciprocity and little perception of shared benefits from certain forms of CSBMs in the area. How, for instance, are arms reductions handled between large Powers and much lesser Powers? The larger Powers will in any case be left with a preponderance of military might over the smaller ones.

Further, the strategic environment in the Asia-Pacific region ought to be addressed. It has become more fluid and dynamic during the past two years. This is of course true for many other parts of the world as well. Certainly we are not sure where we are heading in terms of the strategic scenario in the region. It is uncertain whether it will become unipolar, with the United States dominating everything, or whether it might be bipolar, at least in certain subregions of Asia and, particularly, North-East Asia, or multipolar. In many parts of Asia and the Pacific the strategic scene is going to become predominantly multipolar. Among the strategic changes that have just taken place during the last two years, are the Soviet reductions and pull-back, the reduction in the United States role and the presence and increasing emergence of regional Powers in the area. These developments may have both positive and negative effects on the climate for CSBMs.

Notably, despite an all-round improvement in relations between the countries in the area, particularly in South-East Asia and East Asia, in South Asia serious problems remain unresolved and, with regard to Japan and the Soviet Union, there is the problem of the Kurile Islands. Elsewhere in the subregion there have been dramatic improvements in inter-State relations and also improvements in relations between the regional States and the two super-Powers.

Of course, while there is *detente* between the Russia and the United States, there is also *rapprochement* between the major Powers: the United States and China, the Russia, China and the Republic of Korea, and Japan and the Democratic People's Republic of Korea. China and Viet Nam have improved relations and, also in South-East Asia, China has renewed diplomatic relations with Indonesia and established diplomatic relations with Singapore. Relations are also improving among the Indo-Chinese countries, particularly between Viet Nam and the ASEAN countries.

These developments, again, have had a mixed impact: on the one hand, they reflect a relaxation of tensions in many parts of Asia which will be conducive to at least certain forms of CSBMs. On the other, they have been accompanied by an increase in nervousness and a sense of insecurity in some countries and also by concerns about a rise in intraregional tensions which have hitherto been suppressed as a result of perceived common threats or problems.

In the case of the ASEAN countries, for instance, the Cambodian question was a unifying factor, which gave birth to numerous regional cooperative ventures, but, as the Cambodian problem recedes, the intraregional tensions among the ASEAN countries themselves may rise to the fore. This will surely have implications for CSBMs in the subregion—however, not necessarily negative ones. It could provide an impetus for more CSBM measures, and in fact that is what seems to be happening among the ASEAN countries.

Unlike in Europe, where the situation soon stabilized after the war, in Asia there have been innumerable post-war conflicts and multiple centres of conflict, just as there has been a multiplicity of power centres. The levels of this conflict and tension have varied widely, covering a whole range from hot wars to internal conflicts to intense or moderate bilateral confrontations and tensions. The existence of hot wars and an intense degree of confrontation, in certain cases, make the climate unfavourable for a CSCE-type accommodation in Asia and the Pacific.

But this does not preclude the potential for certain similar CSBMs in areas where conflict is either reduced or very much under control.

There are a few notable cases where either military expenditure is being reduced, or where selective, limited reductions in military capabilities, often unilateral, are being carried out. But the general trend, especially for smaller Powers with the financial wherewithal to increase their military capabilities, is one of increase. The highest levels of expenditures on arms next to Europe are found in this region, particularly in recent years.

As such several factors drive this phenomenon. One is national ambition. There are countries which are newly rich or otherwise have the wherewithal and want to play a larger role in the region. Therefore they perceive themselves as needing the necessary military sinew to play that more dominant role. Another factor is that many countries in the region are starting from a very low military base and building it up. They have not yet attained what they consider for themselves to be reasonable sufficiency. And then there is of course modernization and replacement of equipment. Yet another factor has been the extension of exclusive economic zones (EEZs) at sea, which have vastly increased their areas and created a need for many countries to strengthen their navies.

There have also been modifications of military doctrines and strategies, from an emphasis on counter-insurgency to one on external defence capabilities. A number of countries in the region which traditionally concentrated upon internal disorder have now pacified their internal areas and are building up conventional force capabilities with an external orientation. There are of course the problems of perceived external threats, and, in some cases, they have been perceived as rising. Some countries are in fact worried about reductions in the United States role or even in the Soviet presence, and are fearful of some of the larger Powers in their areas. As a result of the cutting down of the United States presence there arises the need for sharing the defence burden with the United States: for some countries this is leading to decisions to increase their expenditures. And, finally, there have arisen the factors of competition and of the arms race among countries in the region. All this will have to be taken into account in the negotiation of CSBMs in the relevant subregions.

## Main Characteristics and Potential

All these diverse factors mentioned might give the impression that the environment for CSBMs in the Asia-Pacific region is very unfavourable. This is not necessarily so. There are constraints, definitely, but there are also possibilities for confidence-building, security-building and confidence- and security-building measures in the region.

First, although CSBMs are sometimes spoken of as something new for Asia and the Pacific, various kinds have actually been applied in Asia, but not of the CSCE type. They have been localized, bilateral, or subregional, and there are many examples of them in the Middle East, in South-East Asia and in Indo-China. Then there are ASEAN, SAARC, the South Pacific Forum, proposals for a zone of peace, freedom and neutrality and a nuclear-weapon-free zone and, finally, the United Nations effort for peace in Cambodia. These include initiatives as well as systems already in place. Some of them of course are more significant in declaratory terms than in actual implementation. But CSBMs are not a new phenomenon in the region, and this should be stressed, although none is equivalent to those under the CSCE.

While legal or institutional regimes are often stressed, it should be pointed out that a feature of CSBMs in Asia is that they tend to be less institutionalized and less formal systems, as reflected, for instance, in some of the measures worked out between China and the Soviet Union.

Thirdly, we should forget about a pan-Asian CSCE-type conference. The sooner this is realized, the better. Given the factors mentioned, it does not appear to be a possibility for the region. We should strive instead for subregional approaches and bilateral CSBM regimes, which would be more in tune with the prevailing situation in the region. We should also, as noted earlier, seek comprehensive security measures rather than military ones, as sometimes there is greater need to focus on political, economic, social and other forms of non-military cooperation than on military CSBM arrangements as such. This approach will provide the greater potential for the reduction of tensions and conflict in the area, and eventually it could lead to military CSBMs as well.

Fourthly, given the nature and problems of the area, CSBM measures would best be modest, incremental and not very detailed or advanced "high-tech" types. The process could in fact start with very basic activities, such as consultation, dialogue and communication among the military in certain areas. The potential exists for new CSBMs or comprehensive security and cooperation types of arrangements in Asia. Again, these should be on a lesser, subregional scale.

**Potential Military Measures**

- Information: the exchange of publications, including programmes of studies; agreements on pre-notification of manoeuvres and military movements; and invitations to observers;
- Training: exchanges of students in military schools; special courses open to foreign students for certain subjects, such as military participation in civilian activities (road construction, disaster relief, etc.); courses for military officers on arms control and disarmament and the economy of defence; participation in activities such as search and rescue;
- Contact: increased military visits and delegations; military contacts in border areas; procedures for the avoidance of incidents and for their handling; procedures for consultations with various purposes, including the limitation of some types of armaments; direct lines of communication among military authorities; joint exercises and manoeuvres; other contacts for institutional purposes, such as health and sports;
- Institutionalization: regional military conferences of South American authorities for the consideration of additional CBMs, various other aspects of security and other issues.

**Political Consultation**

- External debt;
- Integration and other forms of cooperation;
- Meetings of parliamentarians for the identification of ways of restraining arms expenditures, for the promotion of peace and for the reiteration of the principle of peaceful solution of disputes;
- Identification by political leaders of the elements of strategic differentiation and common security for the region and the establishment of policies of "defensive defence";
- Mechanisms for the curbing of drug trafficking and subversion and for joint action in the case of natural disasters;
- Prioritization of development projects that are of interest

to more than one country, particularly in border areas;

- The possibility of the limitation and integration of military industries;
- Incorporation into political programmes of precise definitions of strategic concerns, defence postures and the like.

**Diplomatic Measures**

- Courses on arms limitation and disarmament at training institutions;
- International seminars on relevant issues;
- Establishment of sections at foreign ministries that would specialize in disarmament matters and would be open to visits by diplomats of other countries;
- Political seminars on strategy.

Now we will put light on Korean peninsula and will address all pertinent issues relating to security concerns and confidence-building measures in the region.

# 5

# The Korean Peninsula: Security Concerns and CBMs

Strategic location, rather than wealth, has made Korea the focus of international rivalry since the late nineteenth century. Three of the great nations of the world—China, Japan and Russia—surround Korea. The United States has also become heavily involved in Korea's destiny as an aftermath of the Second World War and the strategic and economic American stake in the Pacific region. The division of the country after the Second World War was a result of super-Power rivalry and ideological differences; it led to the Korean War and the subsequent decades of bitter confrontation. For the Koreans, resolution of their conflict is virtually synonymous with reunification of the country. For other countries, however, there is no compelling argument for reunification, except as a tension-reducing device; indeed, there is some doubt that the Japanese, for example, want to see a neighbour and potential competitor increase its national power.

So far as the international community is concerned, reduction of tension and the avoidance of renewed war are the objectives. The conflict between the Democratic People's Republic of Korea and the Republic of Korea can be regarded as a surrogate for all of Korea's historic difficulties: the economic and social injustice that the Korean people suffered at the hands of their own traditional aristocracy and then of Japan; the trauma of adaptation to modern industrialized society, with values and styles that are perceived as uncomfortable and foreign; the humiliation of foreign invasion and domination; and the split between the communist and capitalist-liberal approaches to nation-building, intensified by the consequences of the Korean War.

**Historical Backdrop**

Coming to historicity, in the nineteenth century, the misgovernment of a senescent dynasty had engendered poverty and social confusion, much as in China, and the Korean army had declined almost to non-existence. Korea sought refuge in self-seclusion; it was in no position to defend itself against the newly aroused imperialist rivalries of its neighbours, Japan, Russia and China. Japan wanted both Manchuria and Korea for resources and living space; Russia wanted ice-free ports and access to the Pacific Ocean; China wanted to preserve Korea as a buffer zone. All three countries sought hegemony over Korea. Japan's triumph in the Sino-Japanese and Russo-Japanese wars enabled it to take over the country in 1905, and to annex it in 1910. In forced submission, the Koreans' bitter resentment towards Japan endured and festered. Its most remarkable manifestation was the unarmed national uprising of 1 March 1919, in support of national independence. The Japanese brutally suppressed it. The Bolshevik Revolution of 1917 was perceived by some Korean nationalists as offering new hope for the revival of their nation through revolution. The ideology of communism was added to terrorism as a weapon for national liberation. The resulting split among Korean leaders between communism and anti-communism, left and right, thereafter plagued the independence movement along with factional rivalries.

Liberated from Japan and occupied by Soviet and American military forces in 1945, the Koreans demanded and expected immediate restoration of their independence. However, they were once again unprepared to organize and defend their country. The Japanese had systematically excluded opportunity for the development of native political leaders or institutions above the village level. Polarization between left and right made national unity exceedingly difficult. Neither the United States nor the Soviet Union had the will or the understanding to bridge the gap.

To replace the Japanese, the United States—with the agreement of the Soviet Union—proposed a four-Power, five-year international trusteeship, which was violently opposed by most Koreans as a perpetuation of colonial status. Disavowed by the United States, which had conceived it, trusteeship became a Soviet negotiating ploy. The three-way imperialist rivalry of the nineteenth century was now replaced by the growing confrontation between the United States and the Soviet Union, which reinforced the existing Korean ideological division between right and left. Despite the universal Korean desire for a united Korea, and the initial commitment by both superpowers to a unified Korean regime, two years of negotiation ended in deadlock.

The United States, despite earlier indications that it would not intervene, determined to resist the northern aggression, with United Nations support. When the United Nations counter-attack swept into the defeated North, the People's Republic of China came to the North's aid. Two years of negotiations concluded with the Armistice Agreement of 27 July 1953. The war left both halves of Korea devastated and at least 3 million soldiers and civilians dead, not to speak of millions more mutilated and disabled. It reinforced the enmity between the North and South Korean regimes. The armistice did nothing to resolve the underlying conflict; nor did the ensuing 1954 political conference at Geneva.

After making rapid economic progress with a centrally planned economy for twenty years after the Korean War, North Korea has encountered increasing economic difficulties. Yet so far, the collapse of the socialist economies of the Soviet Union and Eastern Europe appears to have had little impact on North Korean policies. South Korea, meanwhile, has far outstripped the North on the basis of export-led, government-coordinated capitalism, and seems finally to be achieving political progress as well, after many years of authoritarian rule. At present, the national product of the Republic of Korea is estimated at five to ten times that of the Democratic People's Republic of Korea, with a per capita ratio of as much as five to one. South Korea is twentieth among world nations in terms of national product, and twelfth-largest international trader.

Despite the enormous military power still deployed on both sides of the military demarcation line, the 1953 truce has held, with only minor violations, for nearly 39 years—probably the longest-lasting armistice in history. Nevertheless, unless and until the basic conflict is resolved, an attempt might be made at renewal of the war if either side were convinced of the vulnerability of the other, with the intention of rapidly seizing enough assets and territory to force capitulation to a unified government of all Korea.

Although political and military confrontation between the two Koreas continues, the last few years have seen significant growth in the dialogue between them, if not in mutual understanding. South Korea formally abjured military conquest in 1960. North Korea, despite its military build-up, its attempts to foment a "people's revolution" in the South, and the attempted assassination of South Korean President Park Chung Hee in 1968, joined m 1972 with the South in a declaration of peaceful unification. The specifics of this agreement were soon ignored and violated, and a number of violent actions by the North in subsequent years contradicted it. Yet the agreement is still endorsed by both sides.

Both North and South have put forward proposals for reunification through some sort of confederation, and for reduction of tensions. The proposals have differed fundamentally in that those of the North begin with overarching conferences and committees, while those of the South begin with small confidence-building steps such as trade, communication, and reunions of separated families. Nevertheless, sufficient convergence was achieved so that a token exchange of family members occurred in 1985, and a series of conferences at the prime-minister level began in 1990. In December 1991, agreements were initialled on non-aggression, peace and cooperation and on denuclearization of the Korean peninsula; these were formally signed in February 1992, and joint committees have been established for their implementation.

The military aspect of the inter-Korea confrontation, representing the capability for renewal of the war, is at the centre of concern regarding the tension on the peninsula. The focal points of this concern are the huge number of forces and weapons deployed on both sides; the North's nuclear weapons development programme; the continued presence of United States ground and air forces in South Korea; and the possibility of external involvement, should hostilities resume.

At the sixth Inter-Korean High-Level Talks, held in Pyongyang on 19 February 1992, the Agreement on Reconciliation, Non-Aggression and Exchanges and Cooperation between the North and the South, an epoch-making event and a milestone in the establishment of peace and the reunification of the country, and the Joint Declaration of the Denuclearization of the Korean Peninsula came into effect.

The North-South Agreement and the Joint Declaration have opened bright prospects for the peaceful reunification of the country and elimination of the threat of war. The commitment of the North and the South to reconciliation and cooperation for the sake of reunification has proved that neither foreign Powers nor differences of ideologies and systems could keep our nation separated. Inspired by the sixth North-South High-Level Talks, our nation has taken a valuable first step towards peaceful reunification.

Towards that end, both sides should implement that first Agreement and endeavour to make it fruitful.

President Kim II Sung said:

> "The Government of our Republic regards these historic agreements as precious results of our efforts to achieve the independent and peaceful reunification of our country and will make every effort to implement them."

The most urgent task facing the North and the South is to bring about the reunification of the fatherland and restore peace to the nation. If another war were to break out in Korea, national reunification, not to speak of the very existence of the nation, would be in jeopardy.

Early solution of the problems of peace could save our nation from the threat of a nuclear war, and the elimination of military confrontation could help to bring about national reunification and unity on thé basis of mutual confidence. Now that the North and the South are firmly committed to non-aggression, they have neither a reason to compete with each other nor a need to waste the resources of the fatherland on meaningless confrontation. In conformity with the spirit of the Agreement, the North and the South should put a halt to the arms race and reduce their troops and military equipment. This would be the most reliable guarantee of non-aggression and of the complete elimination of the threat of aggression by either side.

We have made active efforts in this regard, witness the phased arms reduction proposal put forward in July 1987, the comprehensive peace, package offered in November 1988, and the further detailed proposal made in May 1990 by the Government of the Democratic People's Republic of Korea (DPRK). We unilaterally reduced our troops by 100,000 in 1987, and since 1986 we have mobilized 150,000 soldiers of the People's Army to work for socialist economic reconstruction.

The issues of phased arms reduction, confidence-building exchanges of military information and the elimination of nuclear weapons, which are the main elements of the disarmament proposals we put forward, are reflected in the North-South Agreement and the Joint Declaration. The old "armistice" system of the cold-war era should be abolished in order to make way for the creation of a favourable climate for implementation of the Agreement.

Now that the North-South Joint Military Commission, a new body dealing with military affairs, is to be set up, the armistice-supervising regime has lost its original meaning. Moreover, the United States troops ("United Nations Forces") have no reason to remain in South Korea any longer. It is high time for the United States to put an end to its old policy with regard to Korea and adapt to the changed situation.

Since the problem of Korea's reunification is historically linked with the international relationship, the countries concerned should do their part to create a favourable atmosphere for Korea's reunification. In particular, the United States, the party directly responsible for the situation in Korea, should, albeit belatedly, play the role assigned to it in helping to bring about the reunification of Korea.

Now, however, the relationship between the DPRK and the United States is not in keeping with the current trend and the desire of the people, a fact which indicates that there still exist certain problems on the Korean peninsula that are not in accord with the reconciliation and *detente* of the present time.

The collapse of the cold-war structure based on confrontation between the super-Powers helped create the conditions for improved relations between the DPRK and the United States.

If there is to be a change in the international situation

the United States should amend its policy with regard to Korea in order to create a basis for lasting peace on the Korean peninsula. It should not lay down preconditions in the process of putting an end to the hostile relations between our two countries. The DPRK and the United States have no reason to remain hostile to each other just because they once fought against each other. Now that the DPRK has become a Member of the United Nations, die United States should reconsider the status of "United Nations Command" and "United Nations Forces" and take appropriate measures. We are pleased with the successful outcome of the DPRK-United States high-level talks held in New York early this year.

It is our consistent stand that the Korean peninsula should be turned into a denuclearized zone of peace. We have neither the intention nor the capacity to develop nuclear weapons. We value independence more than physical life. We do not refrain from doing what we should do because of pressure from others nor do we do things we should not do.

When the main obstacles to our signing the safeguards agreement with the International Atomic Energy Agency (IAEA) were removed recently as we demanded, and when propitious circumstances and fair conditions for settling the issue of nuclear weapons were created, we signed the agreement in Vienna, on 30 January 1992, in accordance with the terms of the Treaty on the Non-Proliferation of Nuclear Weapons, and we announced publicly that we would accept IAEA inspections as soon as the safeguards agreement was ratified and a written notification of its ratification sent to IAEA in conformity with the relevant articles of the agreement regarding its entry into force.

In accordance with the request of the Deputies of the Supreme People's Assembly, the safeguards agreement between the Government of our Republic and IAEA was examined at the session of the Assembly's Standing Committee held on 18 February, and the Committee decided to submit it to the Assembly for discussion at its session to be held early in April. On 9 April the agreement was ratified.

The North-South Joint Nuclear Control Commission, established to implement the Joint Declaration, will make the necessary provisions for the denuclearization process.

In the future, too, we will carry out our duties under the non-proliferation Treaty in good faith, thereby contributing in a positive way to turning the Korean peninsula into a denuclearized zone, abolishing nuclear weapons and defending the peace and security of Asia and the rest of the world.

The other important thing in ensuring peace on the Korean peninsula is to achieve national reunification. Only when reunification has been achieved can there be enduring peace. With the recent adoption of the North-South Agreement, the necessary conditions have been created between the North and South to put an end to the confrontation that has gone on for almost half a century and to achieve national unity in an atmosphere of reconciliation.

Once a decision has been taken on the formula for reunification, we could say that agreement on the issue of reunification between the North and the South is feasible. Without deciding on the modalities of the reunification, the North and the South cannot, however much they talk about reunification, work together towards the common objective. Now that the North and the South are facing national reunification, they should agree as soon as possible upon the method of reunification and make every effort to bring it about.

Reunification by way of confederation could be achieved

peacefully in the present circumstances. The ideologies and systems are different in the North and in the South of Korea. If neither side is willing to make concessions on its own, reunification should be realized by way of confederation on the basis of one nation, one State, two systems and two governments, with neither side the victor or the vanquished.

It would be unrealistic to advocate reunification under one system while ignoring the stark reality that there are different systems in the North and in the South. Moreover, unification of the systems, in any way, cannot be acceptable to either side inasmuch as it would be based on the assumption that one side had won over the other.

Reunification by way of confederation is a very practical and realistic way of national reunification. Our nation is one nation and cannot be divided. Ours is a homogeneous nation, one that has been living on the same territory since olden times, creating a national culture with one blood and one language.

Though there are different ideologies and systems in the North and the South, the nation is still one and its homogeneity still exists. Its heterogeneity related to the different ideologies and systems that have existed for more than 45 years is not a major problem when we consider the national homogeneity that has been consolidated throughout thousands of years. The differences in ideologies and systems cannot be either a condition for separating a nation into two parts or an obstacle that cannot be overcome on the road to reunification.

Insisting only on the "reunification of systems" without taking account of such practical circumstances and possibilities would indicate opposition to reunification and the intention of protracting the division. Reunification through the victory of one side over the other would only deepen the North-South confrontation and lead to a military conflict and even the national tragedy of a fratricidal war.

Taking these points into consideration, we advocate reunification by way of confederation on the basis of one nation, one State, two systems and two governments. We are convinced that national reunification can be achieved peacefully and most rapidly if this principle is observed.

We have already put forward a proposal for the establishment of the Democratic Confederal Republic of Koryo as a means of reunification that is in conformity with this major principle. This proposal can serve as the groundwork for a national agreement and certainly as a means of reunification.

The South Korean people and many people throughout the world support our proposal for confederation. Reunification through confederation could be achieved by vesting the regional autonomous governments of the Confederal Republic with more rights on a tentative basis and then increasing the functions of the central government in the future.

North-South dialogue on the process of national reunification should involve a comprehensive negotiation in which not only the authorities of both sides but also broad political forces would participate. The authorities of the North and of the South, all political parties, social organizations and people in all walks of life should develop bilateral or multilateral contacts and dialogues with a view to convening a political consultative conference for national reunification, one which would truly reflect the will of the entire nation and decide on the manner of national reunification.

Through the recent North-South Agreement, the two sides agreed to recognize and respect each other's system on the common understanding that the relation between the North and South is not a relation between States but one within the nation, involving phased arms reduction and cooperation with a view to promoting national unity.

In our view, the historic documents recently agreed are valuable achievements on the road to independent and peaceful reunification of the fatherland and we will make every effort to implement them.

The Korean peninsula, which has been an area of sharp confrontation, is now joining in the present trend towards *detente* and peace.

The signing of the Agreement on Reconciliation, Non-Aggression and Exchanges and Cooperation between the North and South and the Joint Declaration of the Denuclearization of the Korean Peninsula, and the recent suspending of the "Team-Spirit" Joint Military Exercises definitely show that a step has been taken towards peace, m any case, the North and the South should neither halt nor reverse this positive trend, but should rather redouble their efforts to remove military confrontation as soon as possible and to achieve a durable peace. The South Korean authorities should stop the "Team-Spirit" Joint Military Exercises not only this year but for good and should take epoch-making measures to discontinue all other large-scale military exercises.

In the future, as in the past, we shall continue to maintain our peace-loving position and make every possible effort to remove the tension between the North and the South in accordance with the spirit of the North-South Agreement and to turn the Korean peninsula into a denuclearized zone of peace.

## Seoul on Peace and Security on the Korean Peninsula

In his annual New Year's address in 1990, President Roh Tae Woo of the Republic of Korea, then in the middle of his term of office, stated that the 1990s would be the decade of hope, suggesting a bright outlook for the security environment of the Korean peninsula and inter-Korean relations. Indeed, there have been a series of positive developments on the Korean peninsula over the past two years.

**Latest Developments**

Four major developments characterize the recent security environment of the Republic of Korea. First, the establishment of diplomatic relations between Seoul and Moscow in September 1990 generated a wave of change on the Korean peninsula. Seoul's primary goal in normalizing relations with Moscow was to enhance its security and legitimacy *vis-a-vis* Pyongyang. This has been pursued under the name of *Nordpolitik,* a policy which has produced some spectacular successes in the past few years. Seoul has established diplomatic relations with all of the Eastern European countries and the former Soviet Union and has set up a semi-official trade office with China. Seoul-Beijing relations have yet to be normalized, but the only question that remains is one of timing.

Seoul's successes in *Nordpolitik* have prompted Pyongyang to begin to adjust to the rapidly changing world, and have facilitated the phenomenon of "cross-recognition" of the two Korean States by the major international Powers. When cross-recognition of the two Koreas is achieved by the major Powers concerned, peace and security in North-East Asia will be further assured and multilateral dialogue on regional issues could develop.

Secondly, the admission of the two Koreas to the United Nations on 17 September 1991 marked the culmination of the changing international environment. In particular, the decision of the Democratic People's Republic of Korea to join the United Nations signified a major departure from its long-held position on the issue and could signal other possible changes in the direction of North Korea's foreign policy. North Korea had consistently objected to the granting of admission of the two Koreas simultaneously or to each separately, contending that such admission would perpetuate the division of Korea—even though the two Germanys and the Yemens were unified despite their separate membership in the United Nations. The simultaneous entry of the two Koreas into the United Nations is an important symbol of the thawing of the cold war on the Korean peninsula. The parallel membership of the two Koreas could provide a new momentum for the normalization of relations and the ultimate reunification of South and North Korea. Seoul can help Pyongyang come out of its self-imposed isolation by supporting its membership in such United Nations-affiliated organizations as the International Monetary Fund, the World Bank, and the General Agreement on Tariffs and Trade (GATT), in which the Republic of Korea has already been playing a significant role.

Thirdly, with the emergence of East-West *detente* at the global level, the reduction of the United States forces on the Korean peninsula seems inevitable. In accordance with the Nunn-Wamer amendment to the Fiscal 1990 Defense Authorization Act, the United States has begun to draw down its ground troop presence and modify command structures to move from a leading to a supporting role for its forces in the deterrence of war on the peninsula. The military presence of the United States in the North-East Asian region will eventually be transformed into principally a substantial air and naval presence.

Since the United States is a maritime Power and the former Soviet Union is a great Eurasian Power, it seems very difficult for them to reach any kind of agreement on arms reduction in North-East Asia. However, the two countries do share the need to keep peace on the Korean peninsula and are taking a common stance in support of the North-South dialogue. In particular, the United States is encouraging the arms control process led by South Korea so as to ensure that the reduction of American forces on the peninsula will not lead to military instability or to a reckless arms race between Seoul and Pyongyang. The United

States believes that the one place in East Asia where European-style confidence-building measures—and, in time, arms reduction initiatives—seem relevant is in Korea. With the cooperative relationship between the United States and the republics of the former Soviet Union, there is a growing chance for Koreans to secure peace and solve the unification question.

Fourthly, and most important, there have been two developments on the Korean peninsula widely hailed by the South and the North as major progress in inter-Korean relations: one is the adoption of the Agreement on Reconciliation, Non-Aggression and Exchanges and Cooperation between the South and the North—appropriately known as the "Basic Agreement"—at the fifth round of the South-North High-Level Talks on 13 December 1991, and the other is the Joint Declaration of the Denuclearization of the Korean Peninsula, agreed on the very last day of 1991. Both agreements came into effect on 19 February 1992, at the sixth round of the High-Level Talks.

The South-North Basic Agreement is the first official document governing basic inter-Korean relations consented to by the two Korean Governments. It covers three basic areas of inter-Korean relations: political, military, and multifaceted exchange and cooperation, overcoming sharp differences in past positions. For its part, the Joint Declaration stipulates, among other things, that neither side would possess nuclear reprocessing and uranium enrichment facilities and that a joint nuclear control commission should be established, mandated to carry out inspection to verify that the Korean peninsula is nuclear-free.

The entry into force of the agreements explicitly confirms the opening of an era of peaceful coexistence between the two Koreas. As an institutional and conceptual starting-point for the inter-Korean system of cooperative relations, the agreements are to transform the present armistice regime into a solid peace structure on the peninsula. Moreover, the significance of the agreements is manifold. Among other things, if they proceed as they are meant to, the agreements will contribute greatly to the improvement of inter-Korean relations, and will lay a firm foundation for the process of peaceful unification of the peninsula. At a subregional level, the agreements will also go far towards making the area a safer and more peaceful place.

## Security Interests

It is pertinent to note that the security interests of Korea lie in building peace and prosperity on the peninsula and throughout the globe and in the unification of the peninsula. More precisely, it is in Korea's interests to establish a peace system on the Korean peninsula; non-proliferation of nuclear weapons; regional stability; and peaceful unification of the peninsula.

Reducing the risk of war and establishing a permanent peace structure are in the vital interest of the Republic of Korea. Since the legacy of the Korean War still remains and since significant military asymmetries continue to exist along the demilitarized zone, there is a real danger of renewed armed conflict and confrontation. In these tense circumstances, nothing is more important than preventing renewed conflict from occurring, and transforming the existing precarious armistice into a solid peace structure. Against this backdrop, Seoul has vigorously pursued inter-Korean *rapprochement* as was envisaged in the South-North Basic Agreement.

As already mentioned, the Agreement is the most significant step in establishing a peace system between the two Koreas and it could put an end to the four-decades-long inter-Korean confrontation. The Agreement provides that both sides shall recognize and respect each other's system, and endeavour together to convert the present armistice into a durable peace. However, written pledges alone will never bring peace. Sincere and smooth implementation of the Agreement is the key to genuine peace and reconciliation.

**Non-Proliferation of Nuclear Weapons**

Remarkably, in establishing a solid peace system on the peninsula, the Republic of Korea has some immediate security concerns. The most urgent relates to North Korea's nuclear programme. For the past several years, Seoul has identified North Korea's nuclear weapons programme as the greatest threat to peace and stability on the Korean peninsula as well as in North-East Asia.

According to information from various sources, North Korea is rapidly gaining the capability to produce nuclear warheads. To prompt Pyongyang to end its nuclear weapons programme, President Roh Tae Woo issued, on 18 November 1991, the Initiative for Denuclearization and Peace on the Korean Peninsula, and one month later, on 18 December, announced that there were no nuclear weapons in South Korea. The two Koreas consequently adopted the Joint Declaration of the Denuclearization of the Korean Peninsula, mentioned above.

Under the Declaration, the two Koreas agreed to ban the possession or development of nuclear weapons and to allow inspections of suspected nuclear facilities. They also agreed to form a joint nuclear control commission to oversee such inspections. In addition to this development, Pyongyang recently signed and ratified its long-delayed safeguards agreement with the International Atomic Energy Agency.

North Korea should open its nuclear operations to outsiders and accept not only IAEA inspections under the safeguards agreement, but also South Korea's "challenge" inspections as a complement. Pyongyang should realize that elimination of its nuclear weapons programme will promote peace on the Korean peninsula and in North-East

Asia as a whole. It is the duty of the international community not to allow Pyongyang to acquire nuclear weapons and become a potential source of nuclear-weapon technology for other countries.

Regional stability in North-East Asia is crucial to Korean security. A balance of power and interests among the four major Powers surrounding the Korean peninsula is indispensable to peace and stability in Korea and the North-East Asian region. As Korea has frequently been a victim in great-Power rivalries in the past, Korean security depends on the emerging of a stable regional environment among China, Japan, the Commonwealth of Independent States (CIS) and the United States.

The presence and forward deployment of the United States troops in Korea, in particular, serves the role of balancing other Powers and especially constraining Japanese military ambitions, for no other Power can play the role of "an honest broker and the final guarantor of security" without threatening Korea.

China and the republics of the former Soviet Union, for their part, as neighbouring countries that have historically maintained interests in the Korean peninsula, can also play an important supporting role in promoting the peace and stability of the Korean peninsula. Their contribution in this regard will serve the interests of all concerned. Seoul is seeking mutually beneficial relations with these countries on the basis of the principle of reciprocity.

Ultimately, Korea's security cannot be ensured without peaceful unification. The two Koreas have ruled out war or "absorption" as a means of unification and are groping for a truly peaceful method of unification. By the term "truly peaceful method" we mean unification through dialogue and agreement between the two sides, as articulated in the South-North Basic Agreement.

Peaceful change in North Korea is also in Seoul's security interests and it is more desirable than violent change as a means to achieve unification. The unification process in this sense must proceed in ways that will not create any instability on the Korean peninsula and in the North-East Asian region.

# 6
# Arms Control in the Korean Peninsula

For achievement of the peaceful unification of the Korean peninsula, arms control is imperative. A peace system without any military confidence-building measures or any arms reduction between the South and the North would be unstable and vulnerable.

Remarkably, the South-North Basic Agreement contains various measures of confidence- and security-building and arms control with the goal of ending the costly arms race and confrontation between the two parts of Korea. For instance, article 12 of the Agreement provides that the two sides shall "discuss and carry out steps to build military confidence and realize arms reduction, including the mutual notification and control of major movements of military units and major military exercises, the peaceful utilization of the Demilitarized Zone, exchanges of military personnel and information, phased reductions in armaments including the elimination of weapons of mass destruction 'and attack capabilities, and verifications thereof.

The Agreement specifies that a telephone "hotline" shall be installed between the military authorities of the two sides to prevent the outbreak and escalation of accidental armed clashes and a joint military committee shall be established in order to discuss concrete measures for the elimination of military confrontation. To initiate and assure arms control on the Korean peninsula, such measures as those listed above should be implemented as early as possible.

On the basis of the faithful implementation of these confidence-building measures, further steps for effective arms control—that is, control of the structure of the military forces—can be explored.

Generally, there are three important ways to control the structure of military forces: freeze, limitation and reduction. Freeze is the concept of limiting forces and armaments to current levels or to the levels that existed at a specific date. A freeze can be applied when there is parity in the military balance between conflicting forces. On the Korean peninsula, however, there is a significant disparity in the military balance between the North and the South. Hence, this approach is not relevant for the peninsula.

The major drawback in the concepts of a freeze or limitations is that arms control on the Korean peninsula should result in reductions, that is, structural control of the armed forces on the peninsula should take a reduction-oriented approach, aimed at securing a balance through achieving parity in military strength at lower levels.

For effective arms reduction between the two Koreas, the following working principles and objectives need to be considered.

1. The final objectives of arms reduction should be the strengthening of stability and security on the Korean peninsula through the establishment of a stable and secure balance of defensive forces at appropriately lower levels.
2. An initial stage of the phased reduction should eliminate disparities on the higher side so that parity at levels substantially below present levels of the lower side could subsequently be established.
3. In the establishment of mutual agreement on the appropriate level of military strength to be maintained in the subsequent stages, the need for self-defence as an independent unified nation should be satisfied,

taking into consideration the geostrategic location of the Korean peninsula, the history of foreign intervention, and the changes in the surrounding environment.

4. As a matter of high priority, the capability for hunching a surprise attack and for initiating large-scale offensive action should be eliminated, together with the reduction of weapons of mass destruction.
5. Overall levels of offensive equipment such as tanks, artillery and armoured personnel carriers, which are verifiable and which are central to the seizing and holding of territory, must be radically reduced in the first stage of reductions.
6. The number of troops may be reduced in accordance with reductions in armaments and equipment.
7. The reserve forces may be reduced in parallel with the reduction of regular forces.
8. Foreign military forces may be gradually reduced and withdrawn in accordance with the progress made in the structural arms control between the two Koreas.
9. Compliance with all agreed measures of arms reduction should be verified through an effective and strict verification regime which, among other things, would include on-site inspection rights and the exchange of information. Appropriate sanctions should be applied to non-compliance and violations of agreements.

As previously noted, there has been a series of developments in recent years that have had a positive effect on the security of the Korean peninsula. It is very important for the Koreans to take advantage of this opportunity in the post-cold-war era. In this sense, the first challenge for Seoul is to persuade Pyongyang to fulfil the promises of the two inter-Korean agreements. Pyongyang should also realize that written pledges alone will never bring peace or unification. Upon the sincere and complete translation of the agreements into action, the two Koreas can cultivate more areas of common interest, including arms reduction on the peninsula.

At this moment, the most urgent task for Seoul is to solve the problem of North Korea's nuclear weapons programme. As long as the threat of nuclear war persists, it will be impossible to move even one inch towards reconciliation, peace, exchanges and cooperation between the South and the North. Seoul needs to manage its cooperative efforts with the international community effectively so that Pyongyang will eventually be persuaded to give up its nuclear programme.

The four-nation Neutral Nations Supervisory Commission established by the Armistice as a control mechanism still maintains a token presence in the demilitarized zone separating the two sides, but it was deprived of any significant capacity to inspect or verify. The Military Armistice Commission, set up under the Armistice to monitor compliance, has maintained communication between the two commands, although its nearly 500 plenary sessions have served chiefly as a propaganda sounding-board. It has failed to prevent the remilitarization, on both sides, of the four-kilometre width of the so-called demilitarized zone. North Korea has proposed the expansion of the Neutral Nations Supervisory Commission to enable it to verify arms reductions; yet it has resisted all proposals to discuss arms control measures in the Military Armistice Commission, insisting rather upon negotiation directly with the United States and South Korea.

Until recently, North Korea demanded the elimination of United States forces as a precondition for discussions of arms control and other tension-reduction proposals. However, the South regards them as important for security. Although the Soviet Union, before its dissolution, and China up to the present have both publicly supported the North Korean position, both countries as well as Japan have privately considered the continued presence of United States forces a useful deterrent to hostilities by either Korean side.

South Korea's capital region, with a quarter of the population and up to half of its industrial and economic strength, lies within two minutes' jet flying time of the front lines. A massive, highly organized North Korean thrust might succeed in moving south of Seoul to the Han River before the defence could hold it, thus greatly altering the balance of power between North and South. The heavily mechanized United States 2d Division, equipped with the most modern weaponry and constantly maintained in peak battle-ready condition, could make the difference in holding the line north of Seoul, and its participation would guarantee that of United States air and naval forces, which would be even more necessary for a successful defence.

The North Korean nuclear weapons programme is currently the most worrisome aspect of the military confrontation. It presumably began some years ago, before North Korea suffered loss of support from the Soviet Union and China and encountered its present economic straits. It must have siphoned off a considerable amount of North Korea's economic resources. South Korea, also, took covert steps towards a nuclear weapons development programme in the mid-1970s, but was dissuaded by the United States: the North Korean programme may have begun in the same time-frame, and may have been inspired by genuine fear of invasion, in view of mounting South Korean military power, and the changing international alignment demonstrated by the United States opening to China, as well as by the quest for power and prestige.

The North has for years called for a Korean nuclear-free zone, and has repeatedly asserted that its nuclear programme is purely for peaceful purposes, but most analysts seem satisfied that this claim, like other North Korean protestations for propaganda effect in the past, is fake. Objectively, it is hard to see what real advantage North Korea would gain from the development of one or a few nuclear weapons that would offset the financial, diplomatic and moral costs; but the same could be said of North Korea's bombing of a South Korean airliner in 1987.

If hostilities were to resume, both North and South Korea would look to their respective allies for support. Both China and the Soviet Union signed treaties of mutual assistance with the DPRK in 1961. There has always been the possibility that North Korea might mount another attack on its own, then turn to its friends for needed support of a *fait accompli.* This possibility has been greatly reduced in recent years, as the support of both of North Korea's neighbours has declined.

South Korea is linked with the United States through the Mutual Defense Treaty of 1954 and through the presence of American combat forces in Korea. There is also a tenuous link with 15 other nations that participated in the United Nations Command, since a shadow United Nations Command still exists, and a joint statement by the 16 member nations in July 1953 says that in the event of renewed attack, "they would not be slow to resist". Japan would also be involved, because American bases there would be utilized for support; advance consultation with Japan for such use would be required.

The military effort has strained the economies of both sides ever since the Armistice of 1953, with the North apparently putting a quarter of its national product into it, against a sixteenth for the South (although in absolute amount, the annual defence spending of the South has probably surpassed that of the North). The North's military effort must surely be at the upper limit of its economic and human capacity, especially now that concessionary military aid from its allies has largely ceased. The South's military budget is also constrained by newly vocal public opinion.

These limits, and restrictions on supply of advanced weaponry imposed by foreign suppliers—chiefly the United States and the Soviet Union—constitute a sort of arms control.

Neither the Republic of Korea nor the United States has responded positively to the North Korean proposals, nor has either advanced any proposals of its own, except in the area of confidence-building measures. The United States has pointed out that an existing mechanism—the Military Armistice Commission set up under the Armistice Agreement in 1953, which has representatives of both Koreas, China, the United States and other Members of the United Nations involved in the Korean War—could discuss such proposals. The position of both countries has been that North Korea can signal its intention by modifying the offensive deployment of its armed forces and accepting confidence-building steps such as reciprocal observation of military exercises. Offensive deployment, together with North Korea's long record of attempted infiltration, subversion and assassination, and its calls for popular revolution in the South, are taken as evidence that the North's proposals are propaganda rather than substance. South Koreans recall that the surprise North Korean attack of 1950 was preceded by appeals for peaceful unification and offers to exchange political prisoners. In fact, the whole history of inter-Korean proposals and counterproposals aimed at reunification and reduction of tensions is very reminiscent of the long-drawn-out and often fruitless history of arms control and disarmament negotiations between the super-Powers.

In the Korean peninsula, also, it is probable that arms control measures will result from or accompany, rather than lead to, the reduction of tensions. Economic constraints may also force military reductions, but the lessening of suspicion on the two sides is a key factor. Both considerations relate chiefly to the situation within Korea itself. At the same time, both Korean States are dependent upon outside sources for their most sophisticated weapons, and would also be dependent upon outside sources of resupply—especially the supply of oil—if a renewed war were to last more than three to six months. A United States infantry division, an air wing, and support troops support the defence of the South, and would be involved in renewed hostilities. The international community therefore has considerable potential leverage for bringing about arms control in Korea if the concerned nations agree among themselves upon the levers to apply. If, as now seems possible, a significant lowering of tensions is achieved, arms control measures will become practicable as well as important for the continuation of the process of *detente*. The obvious first step, as South Korea and the United States have proposed, would be to provide means of mutual reassurance to both sides against hostile intentions through an exchange of military observers, advance notification of major military movements, and liaison between the headquarters of the two sides by means of an open telephone line ("hot-line").

Such steps were taken in Europe as the beginning of a process of mutual and balanced force reductions, before the dissolution of the Soviet Union. So far none of these proposals has been implemented in Korea, although the Agreement signed between the two Koreas in December 1991 did include establishment of a "hot-line" and notification of major military movements. Like the former Soviet Union, North Korea probably regards secrecy as a strategic asset. Another category of initial measures would include redeployment of forces in defensive, rather than offensive, positions. The United States and South Korea took a unilateral step in this category by cancelling the annual joint "Team Spirit" military exercise for 1992.

At a later point in the process of *detente,* reductions of forces and weapons will receive serious rather than propaganda attention, in order to lessen the military threat and the burden on the economies of both North and South. The critical factors in reaching agreement, in addition to the building of sufficient mutual trust, are practicability, verification of reductions, maintenance of military balance between forces of different composition and armament, and assurance that Korea—either divided or united—can defend itself against possible future outside attack, however unlikely that may appear at present. In this category of arms control measures, also, the United States and South Korea have taken the lead by removing American nuclear weapons from the country and by offering to permit inspection by the North to verify their removal. As mentioned above. North and South Korea have signed an agreement to keep the peninsula nuclear-weapon free, and have agreed in principle to an inspection regime, but no specific actions have been taken beyond the organization of a joint committee. At the same time. North Korea has ratified an agreement with the International Atomic Energy Agency to permit inspection of its nuclear facilities.

In addition, the United States is removing 7,000 troops from South Korea, although plans for further down-sizing were suspended because of the nuclear weapons problem. Other specific categories of weapons could be reduced, if not eliminated, on both sides, as is the case under current United States-Soviet treaties. However, when negotiations between the two sides reach this stage, the need for a balance of forces may necessitate discussion of mutually acceptable mixes of forces and weapons and means for verifying the achievement and maintenance of agreed limits—in other words, a process somewhat similar to the discussion of mutual and balanced force reductions in Europe. The role of foreign forces is an important one in the tension-reducing process; they can be both an additional source of security and a potential security threat. Clearly, North Korea regards the elimination of United States forces in South Korea as a major objective. Although the South Korean Government and the majority of its people favour the retention of United States forces for security, many South Koreans, also, would be glad to see United States troops depart if there were alternative means of assuring security.

The United States has already pledged to withdraw its forces if the Koreans so desire, although the presence of United States forces in South Korea has been regarded as a significant element in the projection of United States power in the Pacific region. North Korea has already suggested the expansion of the Neutral Nations Supervisory Commission as a means of verifying arms reduction measures. An expanded NNSC, or some other international peace-keeping force within the demilitarized zone, could reassure both Koreas against attack, as an alternative to United States forces. Such an international force might be less offensive to Korean nationalist feelings than a continued United States presence.

Aside from the United States forces in South Korea, there are other non-Korean forces to consider for the future: the 249,000 members of Japan's Self-Defence Forces, the large armies of China and the Soviet Union, and United States forces deployed in the Pacific area. While no one of these countries constitutes a military threat at the present time, it would be prudent for Korea not to be defenceless, as it was in the late nineteenth century. As noted, the North has already put forward a proposal for a phased three-year reduction down to 100,000 troops on each side. The proposal has several unrealistic elements, including the low target force levels; future levels for a unified Korean defence would certainly be no lower than Japanese military strength, and should probably be greater in consideration of Korea's land boundary with China and Russia.

However, it would seem useful for the South Koreans to agree to a discussion of the proposal as a test of the North's sincerity in making it, and perhaps as a point of departure for eventual agreement. To encourage and facilitate movement towards reduction of tensions and arms control in Korea, the time may well have come for a conference among representatives of the four countries chiefly involved in Korea's security—China, Japan, Russia and the United States—and the two Koreas. Such a conference—which could go beyond a single meeting and become a standing forum for discussion—could deal, not only with the Korean problem, but with other security problems of the North-East Asian region as well.

It is pertinent to note that the current series of talks between North and South Korea leads to specific, tangible steps towards the reduction of tensions, the resultant atmosphere might be conducive to an international conference. The agenda might include the discussion of transitional peace-keeping arrangements, taking the place of the United States ground forces in South Korea; control of the export of armaments to Korea; and the provision of sophisticated technical means for verification of arms control agreements developed in inter-Korean negotiations. It is possible, also, that the fact of amicable consultation among Korea's neighbours might itself encourage better communication and understanding between North and South Korea.

The year 1991 was an extraordinary one in contemporary Korean history. Over the previous 46 years, tension, antagonism, confrontation and even war had pulled the Korean people into an abyss of misery and misfortune. An aspiration cherished by 70 million Korean people, both in the North and in the South, has been to remove tension antagonism and estrangement, to prevent the outbreak of a fratricidal war, to achieve reconciliation and cooperation at an early date and, eventually, reunification. Following the Joint Communique proclaimed by the two sides on 4 July 1972 on the principles of self-determination, peaceful reunification and national unity, and after a series of talks held on and off in secret and in public, the Korean people is about to realize its long-cherished hope.

The United Nations accepted simultaneously the Democratic People's Republic of Korea (DPRK) and the

Republic of Korea as full Members on 17 September 1991. Then, on 13 December 1991, the fifth inter-Korean talks made a significant breakthrough. The Prime Ministers of the two sides signed the Agreement on Reconciliation, Non-Aggression, and Exchanges and Cooperation between the North and the South in Seoul. This wide-ranging pact includes recognition and respect for each other's system, the end of military and political antagonism and confrontation, the conversion of a cease-fire into consolidated peace, the establishment of offices and other specialized committees, a comprehensive exchange between the two sides, and resumed contacts for families that have been separated.

On 31 December 1991, the two sides signed another agreement, the Joint Declaration of the Denuclearization of the Korean Peninsula (see the "Documentation" section of this issue). On 19 February 1992, after completion of their respective legislative procedures, the two Prime Ministers exchanged instruments of ratification of the two agreements at their sixth round of talks in Pyongyang, thereby putting the two agreements into effect. They also signed and exchanged an accord on the establishment of a specialized committee on inter-Korean high-level talks.

During this period, three specialized committees, on politics, on military matters, and on cooperation and exchange, were established. The two sides also agreed to engage in negotiations for the establishment of a joint committee on control of nuclear weapons, a significant symbolic step towards the implementation of the agreements and declarations. The United States and the Republic of Korea stated that they had withdrawn all nuclear weapons in the South and that there were no nuclear weapons left, and they pledged to cancel the annual "Team Spirit" joint military manoeuvre for the time being.

The Democratic People's Republic of Korea took a positive attitude on the nuclear issue and signed a nuclear safeguards agreement with the International Atomic Energy Agency

(IAEA) on 30 January 1992, agreeing to accept IAEA inspection. On 9 April 1992, the agreement was ratified.

At the same time, there was considerable progress in the relations between China and South Korea. Following the establishment of trade offices, China and South Korea signed trade agreements, which resulted in an increase in their economic cooperation and in exchanges of staff. There has been some progress in the negotiations between Japan and the DPRK on the establishment of diplomatic relations, and the DPRK and the United States are both satisfied with the results of their first high-level talks.

All of the above-mentioned events mark a turning-point in North-South relations, indicating that the settlement of the Korean issue has entered a new era. The proposed summit meeting between President Kim II Sung and President Roh Tae Woo and the results of the meeting will pave the way for full reconciliation and cooperation and for the peaceful reunification of the Korean nation, marking a new epoch in Korean history.

As the Korean peninsula is being transformed from a precarious element posing a threat to peace in North-East Asia, Asia and the world as a whole, to a positive factor conducive to peace, the Korean people themselves should make a great effort to prevent any possible retrogression. The successful solution to the following important problems has aroused great concern among the people.

*First, disarmament.* Only when the agreements signed by the two sides are fully implemented and the disarmament is completely carried out can the military confrontation be ended once and for all and overall reconciliation and cooperation be realized. In this regard, the Joint Military Committee formed by the two sides will assume a great responsibility in the future. How many phases should the process of disarmament involve? How many troops should be reduced in each phase? How to guarantee the implementation of these pacts and carry out effective inspections? These problems cannot be settled overnight.

An appropriate disposition of the reduced troops and weaponry, in particular the weapons of mass destruction, should also be worked out. Nevertheless, disarmament is a trend that cannot be halted. Turning hostile armies into forces engaged in peaceful construction and economic development is a fundamental change and will bring great benefits.

*Secondly, transformation of the Korean Armistice Agreement.* According to the 1991 Agreement signed by the two sides, the cease-fire will be transformed into a consolidated peace. This is closely related to the abrogation of the Korean Armistice Agreement, and to the positions and functions of the United Nations and of the countries concerned in the process. It is expected that the two parts of Korea will do a good job in solving this problem through negotiations.

*Thirdly, military relations with foreign countries.* With a change in North-South military relations, the military relations maintained by both sides with big Powers will certainly not remain unchanged. In this respect, military assistance, military cooperation, and agreements on military and security commitments will be affected. The future of foreign troops deployed and of foreign military bases in Korea will be put on the agenda as well.

*Fourthly, reunification.* The prerequisite for reunification is complete reconciliation and cooperation. Before the current agreement was reached, the two sides had, over the years, put forward their respective proposals as to how to realize peaceful reunification. "The Democratic Confederal Republic of Koryo" and "The Confederation of Koryo" proposed by the North and "The National Community of Korea" put forward by the South had their own distinguishing features and in some respects shared common ground. However, these versions had not been totally accepted. The main reason was that preconditions for reunification were not ripe. Today, with the pre-conditions established, a version acceptable to both sides will certainly emerge, and in this period certain transitional measures and corresponding approaches are expected to be taken by both sides.

However, because the agreements cover wide-ranging subjects, it may not be easy to implement them. If misunderstanding, disagreements or disputes occur, this will have a negative effect on the development of cooperation and reconciliation. Moreover, some unexpected incidents cannot be excluded.

All of the above indicates that it will take some time to realize reconciliation, cooperation and, eventually, peaceful reunification.

The public statements and actions by the two Koreas indicate a sincere desire on both sides to promote a smooth realization of reconciliation and cooperation and to prevent any set-back in the way of attainment of their common goal at an early date. People hope that the two sides will cooperate further on the issue concerning the future and destiny of the Korean nation.

# 7

# ASEAN on Security Concerns in South-East Asia and the Pacific

In terms of security, the Pacific region is not so clearly divided as Europe, which since the end of the World War II has been divided primarily between East and West, or roughly between the forces of NATO and those of the Warsaw Pact, apart from some traditionally neutral Powers outside either of the two military alliances.

That is not to deny the fact, however, that the East-West relationship of competition or even confrontation over the past four decades has also had its impact on the region, especially since the outbreak of the Korean War in 1950, which marked the beginning of the extension of the United States containment policy against what was then perceived as the world-wide Communist threat from Europe to the Pacific region. This explains the involvement of a certain number of countries in the region such as Japan and South Korea in north-east Asia, the Philippines and Thailand in South-East Asia, and Australia and New Zealand in the South Pacific in security alliances with the United States, whether on a bilateral or a multilateral basis, against the Communist threat, be it the Soviet or the Chinese.

On the opposite side, though less intensive, less extensive, and not on a multilateral basis, we may note the Soviet bilateral alliance with North Korea and Viet Nam. While some ASEAN countries have continued to be associated with the United Kingdom, Australia and New Zealand in the five-Power defence arrangement, even though without a well-defined perception of a potential source of external threat, a large majority of the countries in the Pacific have remained uncommitted or have opted for non-alignment in their defence and foreign policy.

It is remarkably that changing alignments, meanwhile, both among Communist Powers and between Communist and non-Communist Powers in the Pacific, have proved such a perception of the world-wide Communist threat to be over-simplistic for the region. They have also helped reinforce the diversity and complexity of the question of threat perception among the countries of the Pacific, especially as far as external forms of threat are concerned.

Indonesia and Malaysia in South-East Asia, for instance, have been generally more concerned over the Chinese threat, however defined, than the Soviet threat. Since the Vietnamese invasion of Kampuchea in 1978, however, Thailand, as a "front-line State", has felt more threatened by Viet Nam. And the Kampuchean conflict, being in a sense a reflection not only of the Sino-Soviet dispute but, more important, a manifestation of the Chinese-Vietnamese conflict, has encouraged Thailand to seek an alignment with China, whose *rapprochement* with the United States as well as Japan, beginning in the early 1970s, may have helped to make that alignment a lot easier than it would otherwise have been. At the same time, Thailand has considered the Soviet Union a friend of Viet Nam, thus a friend of an enemy, more of a potential external threat than China, a perception that has been shared also by Singapore.

In fact, security concerns of the countries of the Pacific region, therefore, do relate to a large extent to the great Powers. But while the atmosphere of the cold war has had its impact on the security orientation of these countries, their perceptions of threat to their security have not been confined solely to the non-Communist or anti-Communist division of the world. Indeed, China and the Soviet Union both happen to be big and Communist Powers. Even so, some distinction has been made between these two, especially as far as the countries of South-East Asia are concerned, as in the cases of Indonesia, Malaysia and Thailand referred to earlier. Furthermore, although Japan is an ally of the United States, some countries in east and South-East Asia, including some allies of the United States as well, have continued to be concerned over the possibility of a future threat posed by the re-emergence of Japanese militarism.

The case of Thailand's concern with the Vietnamese threat has been made earlier. Because of past experience, however, there may be some lingering suspicions on the part of such countries as Singapore and more recently Papua New Guinea, of a possible threat posed by their giant neighbour, Indonesia. Thus, as far as external threats are concerned, there is indeed little commonality of threat perception among the countries of the Pacific region, including South-East Asia. Yet it is interesting to note that the Association of South-East Asian Nations (ASEAN), now comprising Brunei Daressalam, Indonesia, Malaysia, the Philippines, Singapore and Thailand, was established more than two decades ago on the primary basis of a common security concern over a certain form of external threat to their national security, as well as to the security of the South-East Asian region as a whole.

This was a perception, commonly shared by its member countries, of possible external interference in the domestic or regional affairs of South-East Asia, which would threaten their sovereignty, national independence and integrity, and the peace and stability of the region. Past experience has shown, however, that external interference, particularly by major Powers, has always been invited or at least made possible by domestic or inter-State conflicts in the region itself. Thus, what was in effect a domestic conflict or a civil war in Viet Nam involved United States intervention that created the Viet Nam War, which, if less directly, in turn involved Soviet and Chinese intervention. Confrontation between Indonesia and Malaysia likewise provided room for external intervention by major Powers that came to the aid of their respective protagonists. The most recent case has been that of the Kampuchean conflict, which invited the Vietnamese invasion, and either directly or indirectly Soviet and Chinese intervention.

The fullest expression of this preoccupation is the ASEAN proposal for the establishment of a zone of peace, freedom and neutrality (ZOPFAN) for South-East Asia. The promotion of regional co-operation within the framework of ASEAN can therefore be regarded as a confidence-building measure of great significance. Through ASEAN regionalism the member States would not only be able to prevent or at least to minimize regional conflicts and endeavour to solve such conflicts by peaceful means, thereby reducing the possibility of external interference, but they would also be able to use their resources for national development, which would otherwise be allocated for defence purposes. In this sense regional co-operation would also imply some degree of regional disarmament and arms control.

Significantly, the pursuit of their national development would enhance their national resilience. This would not only reduce their reliance on external major Powers to ensure their security, but it would also help them to cope with domestic threats to their stability in the forms of subversion and rebellions, to which most of the ASEAN countries, and indeed the countries in South-East Asia and beyond in the Pacific, have been continually exposed. Such subversive and rebellious activities have been motivated by an ideological, particularly Communist, background, by religious, particularly Muslim, fanaticism, or by separatist aspirations. Indonesia, Malaysia, the Philippines, Singapore and Thailand in the ASEAN region, and Myanmar and

Kampuchea in the wider region of South-East Asia, and Papua New Guinea in the South Pacific have all gone through the experience of one form or another of domestic conflict, whatever its motivation. Kampuchea has not been able to solve this kind of problem to the present day. The same is true with Burma. And what has recently happened in Papua New Guinea with the Bougainville affair, as well as the very recent coup attempt in the Philippines against the Aquino Government, has confirmed the common concern among the ASEAN States and other countries of South-East Asia and beyond in the Pacific over the threat to their domestic stability posed by such internal conflicts.

As such, not only regional but also domestic conflicts may provide room for external interference. Whether or not they do, of course, would depend on certain factors. One of these is the extent to which a particular country is linked to the strategic calculations of a major Power. Another factor is the developments in the major-Power relationship. The more competitive and antagonistic that relationship becomes, the more strongly the major Powers tend to engage in interference in the domestic or interstate conflicts among the countries of the region in so far as they are capable of doing so and to the extent that such interference serves their own interests at a given time.

Indeed, in the latter case a major Power might not even hesitate to instigate such a domestic or regional conflict, in which it could intervene for its own strategic or political ends. And such interference, given the antagonistic nature of the major-Power relationship, might involve the regional States in a wider great-Power confrontation.

Great-Power detente—particularly the Sino-United States *rapprochement* beginning in the last decade, and the current Soviet-United States and Sino-Soviet detente—does reduce the possibility of external interference, at least in the military sense. Such detente helps create a more peaceful international climate favourable to the national developments of the countries of the Pacific, including South-East Asia.

It will reduce the possibility of these countries getting embroiled in a great-Power confrontation. That great-Power detente does reduce such a possibility and the threat of external major-Power interference may be attested to by the fact that the conflict situation in Burma, the separatist rebellion in Papua New Guinea, and the conflict situation in the Philippines created by the recently rather frequent coup attempts against the Aquino Government have not indicated any signs of external interference, except in the case of recent events in the Philippines, in which the Aquino Government did invite limited United States intervention, and the continuing conflict in Kampuchea, which has continued to involve the might of external Powers behind the warring factions.

Indeed, such great Powers as the Russia and China are at the moment preoccupied with their domestic problems, particularly political and economic reforms. But there is still some degree of uncertainty as to their future international behaviour once all these domestic problems are over. For another, good-neighbourly relations are not something to be taken for granted but to be continuously fostered through the promotion and expansion of regional co-operation and confidence-building measures. Thus, the ASEAN countries, and it is hoped all the countries of South-East Asia and indeed of the Pacific region, should be able to use and benefit from the opportunity provided by the new international climate marked by a reduction of tension through great-Power detente to foster trade and economic relations so as to enhance their national development. In so doing they would enhance their own national, and thus regional, resilience.

Given the continued reduction of international tension created by the great-Power detente and, as far as South-

East Asia is concerned, given the prospect of the solution of the Kampuchean conflict in the near future, a conflict which has preoccupied the ASEAN and other South-East Asian countries for the past decade, there is no place for complacency inasmuch as another potential source of regional conflicts seems to be looming on the horizon. This is in the South China Sea, where territorial and jurisdictional claims and counter-claims over the islands therein, particularly the Spratleys and the Paracels, involve China and Taiwan, Viet Nam, Malaysia and the Philippines.

Indeed, some armed clashes have taken place over the issues between China and Viet Nam. It does not seem inconceivable that a future conflict involving the various claimants may eventually invite external major-Power intervention as well.

The growing institutionalization of confidence-building among the ASEAN member States in the form of continuous interaction, intercommunication and mutual consultations, the renunciation of the use of force, and the employment of peaceful means for the settlement of disputes may be a model for a future pattern by which the possible emergence of conflicts in the South China Sea may be dealt with.

**Comprehensive Security Needs**

It is pertinent to note that in many countries in the South-East Asian and Pacific region, security concerns have moved further and further away from the more military and defence-oriented perspective to that of the achievement of political, economic and social stability. In the first few years following the Second World War, when many of these countries remained under colonial rule or some form of tutelage by colonial Powers, security issues were primarily viewed as their colonial mentors viewed them. The domination of international relations by super-Power competition symbolized by the cold war led countries in many parts of the world to view security primarily from this perspective.

Consequently, security was equated with defence and military concerns.

As such, in the Association of South-East Asian Nations (ASEAN), for example, the consensus is that their primary security concerns are political stability, economic development and social harmony. A politically stable country would not have the virus of instability to spread to its neighbours. A country that is economically developed would have a high stake in the preservation of a regional order conducive to the sustenance of economic progress and would presumably not engage in military adventurism disruptive of that order.

At the same time, social harmony is an important element of political stability. The same concerns may be said to apply to the mini-States in the Pacific region, States which will never be able to guarantee the security of their population and other resources through military means. Like their ASEAN neighbours they aspire to political stability, economic progress and social harmony as security goals. This does not mean, however, that military and defence concerns no longer enter into their security considerations. They do, but for many of them the primary sources of security concerns remain internal; they are not military or defence in character.

From this angle of security concerns in South-East Asia and the Pacific, attention is focused on selected countries. These countries may be divided roughly between the less developed and the developed. Among the former are the ASEAN countries, Indochina, Burma and the Pacific island countries, and among the latter are Japan, Australia and New Zealand. The security concerns of the latter group are markedly different from those of the former, because of their size, degree of political stability, level of economic development, extent of social cohesion, and the scope of their regional and global commitments. In a rapidly changing world, the smaller countries in the South-East Asian and Pacific region continue to grapple with fundamental political, economic and social issues, long since resolved by their more advanced neighbours.

The last half of the decade of the 1980s saw remarkable changes taking place throughout the world. Not only were there significant improvements in super-Power relations in what had been areas of great conflict and tension such as arms reduction, but remarkable internal changes in socialist societies have transformed the context and perhaps even the texture of international politics to the extent that traditional security concerns of even the advanced countries in the region could change. The conclusion of the Treaty between the United States and the Soviet Union on the Elimination of Their Intermediate-Range and Shorter-Range Missiles—the INF Treaty—in December 1987 provided for the dismantling of all such nuclear missiles and alsc established the most extensive system of arms inspection ever to be accepted by both States.

Super-Power detente influenced the initiation of normalization processes in the relations between the Soviet Union and China, between India and China, and even between ASEAN and Viet Nam. In the Asia-Pacific region, the only major relationship that has, apparently, been little influenced by these general trends is the Soviet-Japanese relationship, which continues to be characterized by caution and suspicion. Part of the reason behind this seems to be the. apparent inability of the United States to develop and initiate a creative and meaningful response to the Soviet initiatives, which inability leads its allies in the region to adopt a "wait-and-see" attitude towards these initiatives.

In totality, however, these developments could mean the emergence of a more benign external environment, in which super-Power competition and confrontation would no longer be the primary characteristics of the international scene, where regional co-operative efforts could be developed or enhanced, and where the maintenance of a lasting regional order could become a shared aspiration on the part of countries which would now be concentrating their efforts and resources on the achievement of internal political, economic and social stability.

ASEAN countries consider internal stability to be their primary security concern. Whether called "national resilience", "comprehensive security" or "total defence", the ASEAN countries believe that military security is a limited kind of security, that genuine security lies in internal stability and strength, and that this can be achieved through the promotion of economic development and social harmony.

In fact, the Indonesian doctrine of national resilience was developed after the institution of the "new order" following the ouster of Sukamo in 1965. It seeks to overcome the inherent weaknesses and vulnerabilities of Indonesia due to the vast archipelagic character of its territory, its location between the Indian and Pacific Oceans, its ethnic, linguistic and religious diversity, its vast and rapidly growing population, and its increasing income disparities. These vulnerabilities could lead to fragmentation and could invite foreign intervention.

Hence, stress is placed on the need to unite the people through the common ideology of Pancha Shila, a strong political leadership with the military, the father of the nation, playing the dual function of military defence and socio-political agent, and a development-oriented, disciplined, nationalist and politically conscious citizenry.

With respect to external security threats, Indonesia considers China, rather than the Soviet Union, to be the major long-term threat to itself and to the region. Consequently, it has been the most cautious among the ASEAN countries in normalizing its relations with China, and until the Thai initiatives in Indochina, the most benign in its attitude towards Viet Nam. Malaysia's comprehensive security posits the inseparability of political stability, economic success and social harmony from national security. Military security, accordingly, is viewed as an insufficient basis for the security of the nation. As Malaysia is multiracial, the achievement of social harmony is considered to be a necessary component of national security. Malaysia also views a secure external environment as a requisite of national security. Such an environment is one that is conducive to, and supportive of, its internal political and socio-economic development.

This comprehensive, or total, approach to security, as well as its internal focus, is common among the rest of the ASEAN countries. In the Philippines, where the Communist insurgency remains the main security threat, the multifaceted and comprehensive character of security is well recognized. The Philippines approach to counter-insurgency takes this into account as it involves the application not only of military power, but also of political, socio-economic and psychological resources to the insurgency problem. In terms of political stability, political succession is a security concern shared by ASEAN countries. As their leaders advance in age, the issue becomes all the more pressing, for while succession mechanisms might be in place, the certainty that they will work is open to question. Even for countries with an overwhelming mandate for the return to constitutional rule, such as the Philippines, the political decay of the previous dictatorial regime continues to wreak havoc upon the political system. Disruptive events such as the six attempts made to topple the Government by *coups d'etat* have characterized the Philippine political situation since the democratic restoration began in 1986.

The process of political succession is a crucial element in the maintenance of stability. Without effective succession procedures, political stability would be seriously impaired as various groups would manoeuvre to gain political power through violent means the moment a power vacuum formed.

Another concern in ASEAN countries is rapid population

growth in the face of uncertain economic development. This is true with regard to Indonesia and still more in the case of the Philippines. Wide disparities between the few rich and the majority poor remain a problem and could trigger or exacerbate social unrest. The revolution of rising expectations could inflict further damage on the social fabric, which is already fragile, especially as regards ethnic communities which perceive the inequalities of the system as being loaded against them.

On the issue of China, Singapore has moved closer to China faster than either Indonesia or Malaysia, but has maintained its policy of recognizing Taiwan *de facto* as a separate country. These differences in the perception of external threats have been an important obstacle to the emergence, not only of a common policy *vis-a-vis* their more powerful neighbours, but also of a common external security strategy among them.

**Other South-East Asian Countries**

While external security concerns continue to remain important, the need to achieve political stability, economic development and social harmony is clearly an important component of national security for other countries in South-East Asia. While Viet Nam continues to view China as a principal threat because of the latter's fraternal ties with the Khmer Rouge in Cambodia, it must nevertheless seek to maintain political stability and economic progress if internal security is to be assured. To this end, Viet Nam appears to be poised to seek economic ties with the West, Japan and ASEAN once again in order to rehabilitate its economy, which had been ravaged by decades of war. Viet Nam needs to look elsewhere than to its partners in the Council for Mutual Economic Assistance because the latter would not be in a position to extend economic support and assistance inasmuch as they are also in the process of internal economic reform and rehabilitation. Besides, the limiting of economic ties to socialist countries has not led to economic progress in the past. There is also greater security to be had in diversifying economic ties with as many countries in the world as possible.

Thus, Viet Nam welcomed the invitation of the Prime Minister of Thailand to turn Indochina "from a battlefield into a market-place". Viet Nam seems prepared to allow the intrusion of free market forces into Laos and Cambodia as well, so long as the process in these two countries does not proceed ahead of that in Viet Nam.

In Myanmar, the immediate task of the military government which succeeded U Ne Win in 1988 was to hold the country together amid political turmoil and violence, a bankrupt official economy and unabated ethnic insurgency. The immediate and main security concerns of the country could only consist of those related to political survival. The military government has allowed a certain amount of economic liberalization in order to ease the burdens of a bankrupt economy. It has also allowed the entry of foreign private capital in the exploitation of its natural resources, particularly Thai participation in teak logging and fishing, joint ventures with foreign groups in export and import trading, and oil exploration and regularization of counter-trade with China.

Whether or not these economic measures would provide a modicum of economic stability to Burma remains uncertain. Equally uncertain is the future of political stability where continued military rule may not be conducive to political reforms, including the holding of fair and honest elections in May 1990. Aung San Suu Kyi, perhaps the most popular opposition figure, noted that the real issue of free and fair elections was whether political and human rights would exist prior to the elections, permitting the free conduct of the campaigns, rather than at the time of the elections.

Ethnic insurgency has also been a security concern

since 1949 when the Karens started their revolt. Meaningful sharing of power could be the key to the resolution of the problem of minorities, one which no government of Burma has so far seriously considered.

Ethnic insurgency is complicated by the drug trade, reportedly the means of financing these revolts. Their persistence does not augur well for economic development inasmuch as defence expenditures would continue to be high as military power continues to be the enforcer of national unity in Myanmar.

## The Pacific Region

### *Japan*

It is significant to note that while Japan subscribes to the doctrine of comprehensive security, its external security concerns command a great deal of its attention. The primary source of external threat remains the Soviet Union, largely because of its continuing occupation of the northern territories and its fortification of some of them. However, historic rivalry with China remains an important consideration in Japanese calculations of security.

The Middle Kingdom syndrome is thought to be only temporarily dormant, and likely to be revived once Chinese modernization plans have been achieved. Because South-East Asia remains one of the most important sources of raw materials and cheap labour, Japan considers the stability of this region to be important to its own security. This region also controls the vital sea lanes of communication through which its oil supplies from the Middle East pass—energy supplies that fuel Japanese industries. Hence, it has maintained an active interest in the economic development and political stability of the region. To this end, Japan has been a major contributor not only to investments, but also to official development assistance and trade for ASEAN and, to a lesser extent, for the other countries in South-East Asia.

In fact, a beneficiary of the security umbrella of the United States in the region, Japan seeks continued American military presence in the Asia-Pacific region, especially because of its assessment that Soviet military strength in the region remains a force for instability. It is generally believed to be likely that the reduction or withdrawal of American military presence would be followed by Japanese rearmament, a development largely unwelcome in South-East Asia and in the south-west Pacific.

### *Australia*

Contrary to laymen's perceptions, Australia has had security concerns because of its isolation from Western Europe, the place of its cultural and social origins. Japan, China and the Soviet Union had figured, at one time or another, as sources of security threats: Japan owing to its aggressive actions during the World War II, China because of the fear of communist contagion, and the Soviet Union because of its competition and rivalry with Australia's American super-Power ally. Among its immediate neighbours, Indonesia was perceived by Australian extremists as a threat, especially after the latter's invasion of East Timor. Australia also views the destabilization of relations between or among its South-East Asian neighbours as a security threat to itself. The unresolved Cambodian issue continues to be part of its security concerns.

Australia is also concerned about the well-being of its small neighbours in the South Pacific. Lacking in human, economic and material resources, they could be susceptible to big-Power manipulation and exploitation. Consequently, it has developed interrelated surveillance systems to protect island nations from predatory distant water fishing fleets; it has concluded an agreement with Papua New Guinea to consult and act to repel external armed attack; and it has increased ship visits to island countries to demonstrate its good will and credibility.

Remarkably, drastic change in the correlation of forces between East and West is also an Australian security concern. The future of the United States military facilities in the Philippine bases could be perceived as affecting this correlation of forces, where the removal of those facilities could tilt the correlation in favour of the East. Similarly, the alliance with the United States and New Zealand (ANZUS) is viewed as a major component of its security, the New Zealand policy of no nuclear ship visits notwithstanding.

### *New Zealand*

Located between Australia and Antarctica, New Zealand has the luxury of not being faced by any threat of invasion or armed attack in the foreseeable future. As only the two super-Powers are considered to have the capability of launching such an attack, and as the probability of such an attack by either of them is very low, if it exists at all, New Zealand's security concerns lie rather in low-level threats and in drastic, changes in its external security environment. The more credible security concerns are terrorism and hijacking, harassment of its sea and air lanes of communication and trade, infringements of its exclusive economic zone, and threats to its agricultural exports.

In fact, New Zealand has also adopted a hard-line policy on the issue of nuclear weapons, for which it incurred American displeasure. The effectiveness and viability of ANZUS became open to question as a consequence of this policy.

### *The South Pacific Island Countries*

Fiji, Kiribati, Nauru, Papua New Guinea, the Solomon Islands, Tonga, Tuvalu, Vanuatu and Western Samoa lie strategically at the geographical crossroads of major ocean routes. Their value lies in this geostrategic location. Although small in area and population and underdeveloped in their economies, their bigger neighbours in the South Pacific have accorded them the status of equals in the South Pacific Forum, the region's symbol and instrument of regional decision-making.

They are small States with small populations, territories and resources. Their inability to protect themselves from predatory distant water fishing fleets and from overt armed attack by hostile external Powers have made them extremely vulnerable and have prompted co-operative action from their larger neighbours. Particularly important is the need to protect their resources from more powerful fishing interests. Many of these States do not possess major resources apart from those derived from the ocean.

Hence, they cannot permit the loss of, or injury to, these resources without serious and dire consequences for their people. The most pressing of their concerns is, therefore, in the area of economic security. One of these concerns is the use of drift-net fishing by foreign fishermen. Involving several vessels in co-operative action, long nets are laid in long lines across the ocean. In many cases they cover thousands of kilometres of ocean where indiscriminate fishing takes place. All kinds of living creatures coming in contact with these nets are trapped and killed, not only depleting fisheries resources, but also depriving small island fishermen of their catch.

Another of their security concerns is the need to forge national harmony in their societies divided by racial and ethnic differences. The case of Fiji is illustrative of the difficulty of creating such harmony in a society with substantial ethnic diversity with broad participation in the political and social systems being necessary to achieve political stability. Another example is that of New Caledonia, for which Forum countries are seeking independence. A satisfactory arrangement under which Kanaks, French settlers and others could live together in harmony remains elusive for that Territory.

The South Pacific has been a site for nuclear testing, and consequently, countries in the region have become sensitized to this issue. In response to this concern, they adopted the South Pacific Nuclear Free Zone Treaty on 6 August 1985, coinciding with the anniversary of the atomic bombing of Hiroshima. The Treaty of Rarotonga, as it came to be known, is binding for its members in a vast area bordering in the east on the area covered by the Latin American nuclear-weapon-free zone and to the south on the demilitarized area of the Antarctic Treaty.

Under the Treaty each party undertakes not to manufacture, or otherwise acquire, possess or have control over any nuclear explosive device; not to assist or encourage the manufacture or acquisition of any nuclear explosive device by any State; to prevent the stationing or testing of nuclear explosive devices on its territory; not to dump radioactive wastes at sea anywhere within the Zone and to prevent such dumping by anyone in its territorial sea.

The Treaty also calls upon the members of the Forum to support the conclusion of a global convention prohibiting the dumping of nuclear waste at sea. Through one of its protocols it also prohibits nuclear testing anywhere in the South Pacific zone.

Further attempts to protect the region's natural resources and the environment included the adoption of the South Pacific Regional Environmental Programme on 25 November 1986. The Programme covers the exclusive economic zones of all Pacific island countries and territories and those areas of the high seas enclosed on all sides by these Pacific exclusive economic zones. The aim of the agreement is to protect the marine environment from pollution from land-based sources, seabed activities, and the storage of toxic, radioactive and other hazardous wastes. Forbidden substances are listed, and in no circumstance are they allowed to be put into the sea. Although the agreement is not applicable to Powers that carry out nuclear testing, its parties are obligated to adopt sound environmental management with regard to the consequences of such testing.

No doubt the co-operation of major Powers such as France, the Soviet Union, the United States, China, Japan and others is a requisite for successful implementation of the provisions of this agreement.

With the collapse of USSR, now major rivalry in the region is between the USA and China. According to a recent news report (Sept. 2010) China is going to set Killer Missiles in the region to protect its maritime interests.

# 8

# ASEAN Countries on Openness and Transparency

The concept of regional cooperation for South-East Asian countries was mooted in the early 1960s amid the tension of the cold war and the rise in military might of both the Soviet Union and the People's Republic of China. Leaders of the South-East Asian countries at the time recognized the need to manage their security situations, both domestic and regional, and they believed that the peace and stability of the region could be fostered by promoting economic, social and cultural development through cooperative programmes. They also believed that regional cooperation in the political and economic areas could enhance stability and safeguard the region against the effects of super-Power rivalry. They decided that the region needed an organization as a forum for dialogue, to find solutions to intra-regional differences as well as to manage relations with the super-Powers, whose presence and interest in the region were substantial.

These ideas were expressed and eventually incorporated into the ASEAN Declaration the Bangkok Declaration, signed in Bangkok on 8 August 1967. Hence the establishment of ASEAN could be regarded as the beginning of a process of establishing CBMs and openness and transparency among its members. ASEAN objectives, as reflected in the Bangkok Declaration, represented the collective will of member Governments to address a major strategic challenge of that time: how to face growing communist insurgencies, internal tensions and civil strife in their countries without being dragged too deeply into East-West conflicts and without disrupting their domestic political and economic agendas.

The response to that political, economic and security challenge was outlined in the Kuala Lumpur Declaration, signed in 1971. The document reaffirmed ASEAN States' political resolve and shared determination to secure the recognition of, and respect for, South-East Asia as a zone of peace, freedom and neutrality (ZOPFAN), free from any form of interference by outside Powers. ZOPFAN was the first indication that a process of openness and transparency was making some progress within ASEAN. Another interesting aspect of ZOPFAN—an indigenously conceived regional security order—was that it allowed and encouraged non-ASEAN countries to associate themselves with the concept and its goals.

By that time, ASEAN leaders and officials had already succeeded in establishing a working relationship based on a flexible framework to accommodate diverse opinions and interests. Although the foundation had been laid for regional security cooperation, there were still no clear institutional programmes or plans of action in either the economic or the political security field.

It is pertinent to note that in 1975 following the withdrawal of American troops from Viet Nam, the political and security equation changed, dividing South-East Asia into two groups, each with its distinct ideological orientation. The region was plunged into a serious conflict that had the potential to destabilize ASEAN. Socialist regimes ruled in Saigon, Phnom Penh and Vientiane. For the first time, members of ASEAN recognized the seriousness of the situation and the urgent need to react to the threat of communism in a more concerted manner.

Nine years after ASEAN's creation, its heads of government finally agreed to a summit meeting in Bali in 1976 to discuss, assess and respond to the alarming security situation.

Remarkably, first ASEAN summit produced two significant agreements, which further indicated the direction of ASEAN cooperation: The Declaration of ASEAN Concord and The Treaty of Amity and Cooperation in South-East Asia. The Concord stated the objectives and principles of cooperation, complete with plans of action in economic and social development, incorporated the members' pledges of mutual assistance in the event of natural disaster and reaffirmed their intention to cooperate in regional development programmes and to develop a recognizable ASEAN identity. The Treaty, on the other hand, provided the framework of political cooperation based on mutual respect for one another's sovereignty, non-interference in the internal affairs of others, and the peaceful settlement of disputes.

The most significant aspect of the first ASEAN summit was the rejection of a military-bloc type of response or a confrontational approach to the threat of communism. The summit highlighted instead the benefits of harmonizing views, coordinating positions, and undertaking common and concerted action, in both intra-regional and extra-regional relations. The emphasis was on the need to enhance economic growth and social development, with the specific aims of achieving social justice, increasing the standard of living of the peoples of ASEAN, and strengthening the national resilience of member countries as well as the regional resilience of ASEAN.

ASEAN countries have chosen an economic-cooperation model, suggesting that members integrate themselves substantially with the global economic system through trade, finance, investment and other international sectors.

Further, in 1977 at the second ASEAN summit, in Kuala Lumpur, ASEAN Heads of Government reaffirmed their commitment to ZOPFAN, the Concord and the Treaty of Amity. From 1977 to 1987, ASEAN countries proceeded to fulfil their commitment to ASEAN cooperation. The scope and nature of their cooperation expanded rapidly, primarily in the political, economic and social sectors. The subsequent ASEAN summit, in Manila in 1987, focused, *inter alia,* on improving the functioning and extent of ASEAN cooperation and joint ventures in industrial projects. Progress was also made in regional security cooperation, as indicated by the introduction of the concept of a South-East Asia nuclear-weapon-free zone (SEANWFZ) in 1984.

In fact, the SEANWFZ proposal was a follow-up to ZOPFAN, with the specific intention of making the region a nuclear-weapon-free zone. SEANWFZ could be considered as ASEAN's contribution to regional arms control and disarmament, particularly in support of the Nuclear Non-Proliferation Treaty (NPT). At the fourth ASEAN summit, in Singapore in 1992, it was decided that the ASEAN Foreign Ministers should look into and elaborate the idea of the SEANWFZ.

Basically, ASEAN's comprehensive security concept covers not only military deterrence and territorial defence components but trade and commercial aspects, including the issues of market access, industrial development and technology acquisition, and the social well-being of individual members. ASEAN regarded comprehensive security as an interlocking system of political, social, economic and military forces that could result in trade-offs and synergistic effects. From that perspective, consideration of CBMs or measures to encourage greater openness and transparency, should not be confined to military or defence-related programmes alone.

A multidimensional approach to managing the challenge of maintaining peace and security and to disarmament should be given consideration and greater encouragement. It is through that multidimensional approach that ASEAN has been able to keep the peace and maintain stability for its members over the 42 years since its creation. Economically, socially and culturally, ASEAN members have progressed and recorded remarkable growth. The confidence gained and the openness and transparency among the members of ASEAN—owing to their cooperative endeavours in the political, economic and social areas—can be considered the major reasons for its success. The confidence gained by ASEAN was not derived from a previously established structure for negotiating and implementing security and defence-related measures, but from persistent efforts to remain outside the balance-of-power game, watching from the periphery with neutrality.

### CBMs, Openness and Transparency

It worth mentioning that a major factor that contributes to CBMs, openness and transparency in ASEAN is the fact that all ASEAN countries are signatories to international non-proliferation agreements such as the NPT, the Biological Weapons Convention (BWC), and the Chemical Weapons Convention (CWC). Apart from supporting the United Nations Register of Conventional Arms. Further, ASEAN countries also adhere to and strictly observe all export control measures on dual-use materials. ASEAN is confident that there is no danger of nuclear weapons proliferation or an uncontrollable arms race among its members.

In fact, the regular habit of cooperation and dialogue, fostered through regularly scheduled meetings, is well institutionalized in ASEAN. Mechanisms include the regular summit meetings of heads of Government; the annual ASEAN Ministerial Meeting of Foreign Ministers (AMM) and Economic Ministers (AEM); special meetings of foreign ministers or economic ministers as and when necessary; senior political and economic officials' meetings (SOM and

SEOM); and a series of other meetings at official and unofficial levels.

ASEAN also has a dialogue process with major and medium Powers through ASEAN Post-Ministerial Conferences (PMC), and a series of ad hoc meetings of experts and officials. Those frequent contacts and consultations have allowed ASEAN governments to develop habits of cooperation, to learn to accept one another and to overcome suspicions and years of hostility resulting from their different historical and cultural experiences. The meetings have contributed extensively to the promotion of understanding and have helped foster good will within ASEAN region..

The Treaty of Amity and Cooperation, ZOPFAN and the SEANWFZ have been key concepts with the potential to build trust and confidence among ASEAN member countries. The concept, as explained in the relevant documents, could lead towards greater regional consensus on security matters for ASEAN. Wider acceptance of those concepts by outside Powers, along with CBMs, openness and transparency, would have a political impact, helping to ensure peace and security for the region.

Simultaneously, specific cooperation in the security and defence fields has been bilateral. That format of cooperation has been extensive and regular. Although not regional in character, such cooperation has nonetheless heightened CBMs, openness and transparency between some members. That format of cooperation could be further expanded for border-control, anti-piracy and anti-smuggling activities. Frequent exchanges of visits between senior military officials have afforded the opportunity for military personnel to establish rapport, exchange views regarding threat perception and familiarize themselves with the defence doctrines of neighbouring countries, and have provided the opportunity for training at each other's defence colleges.

In considering the future prospects for truly region-wide ASEAN cooperation in security and defence, perhaps the question some might ask is the following: If, at the height of the cold war, ASEAN security cooperation was confined to bilateral cooperation among six States, is it conceivable now, after the collapse of the East-West rivalry, that ASEAN as a group could develop a regional security and defence pact? Once Viet Nam becomes a full-fledged member of ASEAN in July 1995, there is absolutely no reason for ASEAN to do so. For the time being, it appears that ASEAN countries prefer informal mechanisms and an informal approach to CBMs, openness and transparency; informality allows for flexibility and freedom of manoeuvre. For ASEAN, CBMs and transparency measures seem to work well in an atmosphere of informality and cordiality.

Such an atmosphere already exists but needs to be nurtured. The challenge for ASEAN, therefore, is to reach consensus on the appropriate mechanism and type of activity to nurture the openness and transparency. Some in ASEAN believe that while the mechanism and activities developed in Europe to address that region's specific geostrategic situation could be useful to ASEAN, others are of the view that Europe's model of CBMs and openness and transparency is not suitable for ASEAN and cannot be applied in an indiscriminate and open-ended manner.

## Contemporary Regional Security Issues

It is well accepted that the collapse of the bipolar power structure of the cold war in late 1989 completely changed the security equation in South-East Asia. East-West ideological antagonism, bloc politics and military confrontation dissipated suddenly and unexpectedly. Erstwhile enemies have mended their relations. Cambodia, Laos and Viet Nam have participated in a limited way in some ASEAN events, thus signalling a new peaceful regional order in the making.

Bug, against this promising outlook, ASEAN members

are being warned of a growing threat and possible aggression from China arising out of overlapping territorial claims in the South China Sea. While many view an external military threat to ASEAN as unlikely, the fact that this other perspective exists in the regional grouping underscores the reality that there is no consensus within ASEAN on the issue. Thus if management of potential conflict in the South China Sea revolves around seeking accommodation between ASEAN and China, the achievement of a consensus resolution within ASEAN will be a difficult process. The tendency of analysts and researchers from certain countries to highlight the new security threat in the South China Sea and to emphasize the need to undertake a series of confidence and security-building measures, as well as weapons-control measures, that resemble the European model, is considered by some to be counter-productive to peace and stability in ASEAN.

Remarkably, among the ASEAN countries there are various views about how the Association should proceed with China. The fact is that ASEAN members are vulnerable, and there may be a tendency to over react. Experience indicates, however, that systematic effort in opposing a major Power, for example, imposition of an embargo or boycott, does little to promote stability and security in the region. On the other hand, there have been enormous changes in China, making it a very different country today from what it was. Its open-door policy has made it a much more congenial neighbour, and that is probably the key to the maintenance of peace and stability, open sea lanes, vigorous trade and investment opportunity in the wider Asia-Pacific region.

To sum up, definition of a security role for ASEAN would help produce a new strategic landscape, one in which ASEAN issues and agendas would be given greater weight. The creation of a new strategic order in an ASEAN-based military alliance appears inappropriate and undesirable. The absence of a common threat perception makes it unlikely for ASEAN to evolve into a defence community.

Instead of focusing on the existence of a security threat to regional peace and security, ASEAN countries prefer to see the evolution of CBMs, openness and transparency, starting with cooperation within the framework of the ASEAN Regional Forum (ARF). In a security environment no longer dominated by cold-war ideological conflicts and extra-regional alliances, the impetus for regional defence collaboration withers.

The launching of the first ASEAN Regional Forum (ARF) in Bangkok generated much interest and high expectations among the members of the Forum and among security analysts in general. Inevitably, the question arose as to why ASEAN members felt the need to set up such a mechanism and whether they intended it to play a central role in the East Asia security regime.

Peeping through recent history, the Asia-Pacific region could be described as a battleground of conflicting interests among external powers and regional States. It underwent colonization, when actions were not always taken in the interests of the region. Settlements of issues and arrangements which affected the countries in the region were concluded mainly by the great Powers of the day. In exceptional cases, regional States were brought in, for example, in the 1954 Geneva Conference or within the South-East Asia Treaty Organization (SEATO). Yet the efforts were never directed primarily towards giving the region a chance to decide and act for itself. The turmoil of the sixties and seventies further showed that internal problems sometimes provided opportunities for major Powers to intervene in localized struggles and conflicts towards ends which were not necessarily in the interests of the region.

During that uncertain period in South-East Asia, ASEAN was formed in an attempt to offer better prospects for peace and stability. While ASEAN professed not to be security-oriented, the reason for its formation was certainly the instability and insecurity of the period. From its early years, ASEAN has been conscious of the need to address security issues. Indeed, its most noteworthy achievements have been political, especially in terms of improved relations between the ASEAN States and their regional partners, brought about despite the many bilateral problems existing among its members at the outset.

Efforts to establish ASEAN on a firm and lasting basis coincided with the Association's collective efforts to assist in the management of the Cambodian problem. That signalled a future role. The late 1970s and 1980s witnessed the direct involvement of ASEAN members, individually and collectively, in the Cambodian peace process. The conclusion of the International Conference on Cambodia in 1991 was significant inasmuch as countries in the Asia-Pacific region, particularly ASEAN countries, participated for the first time on equal terms in the international settlement of a regional issue. For many countries in the region, that involvement was the first experience in negotiating a peace settlement, participating in peace-keeping efforts and monitoring elections. Perhaps most significant of all, countries in the region, large and small, began to learn to cooperate with one another on matters of common concern.

Coming at the end of the cold war, the experience of the International Conference showed that it was possible to ensure that the unfavourable conditions under which regional affairs had often been conducted in the past need not be repeated. It also meant that members of the region could seek jointly to address remaining concerns, such as the rehabilitation of Cambodia, the containment of the potential problems in the South China Sea, the nuclear challenge from the Democratic People's Republic of Korea

(DPRK) and the management of change in the major power relationships in the region.

Although discussions at many ASEAN Ministerial Meetings (AMM) often focused on political cooperation in matters of mutual concern, ASEAN countries were nevertheless aware that security matters and security policy were still not formally on the ASEAN agenda. It was not only the political momentum gained from the Cambodian undertaking and the conditions prevailing at the end of the cold war that impelled discussion on-specific security concerns, but the added impetus of the Leaders' Summit in 1992 in Singapore. At that gathering, the heads of government formalized and endorsed a process already under way.

Further momentum was provided by the growing importance of Asia and the Pacific in the global economy. Leaders in the region became aware that regional instability could threaten that growth and could have global repercussions. At the same time, they recognized that rapid economic growth created interdependencies which could result in vulnerability, especially because of reliance on foreign investments and markets. They accepted the fact that, as nations drew together, free access to markets, unimpeded sea lanes and access to resources were indispensable for further economic progress. They also became aware that those factors could be potential sources of conflict.

Increasing economic interdependence through region-wide trade and investment pointed to the need to talk about security with partners. As economic affluence grew, so did the desire of nations to enhance their defence capabilities and to upgrade defense structures through higher state budget allocations. Such moves could worry neighbours.

So, despite reticence on the part of regional leaders to discuss security matters, steps to create a region-wide security process went ahead. For example, the Foreign Ministers of Australia and Canada, in the early nineties, suggested an organization for Asia along the lines of the Conference on Security and Cooperation in Europe (CSCE) which could be known as the "Conference on Security and Cooperation in Asia (CSCA)". Though the concept was not accepted at the official level, regional "think-tanks" in the non-governmental sector began to explore the merit of having ASEAN discuss security issues through the established regional forums. Deliberations at the governmental and non-governmental levels kept interest alive in creating some form of regional security system and setting a logical time-frame for such an endeavour.

The perceived decrease in the United States military capability in the region following the termination of the United States-Philippines base agreements, taken together with the new post-cold war situation and the emergence of other regional powers, impelled the search for a relevant process. In another closely related development, the United States, in a fundamental change of policy, agreed to consider security aspects from a multilateral approach while maintaining its own bilateral arrangements with countries in the region.

In sum, in addition to various intense regional security concerns, the most important factor in placing security issues on the ASEAN agenda was the increased self-confidence of regional leaders, especially ASEAN leaders. That confidence was brought about largely by unprecedented economic growth and improvement in the overall relations among regional countries. Moreover, ASEAN's involvement in the Cambodian peace process, its tackling of other security issues during ASEAN Ministerial Meetings, Post Ministerial Conferences (PMC) and dialogues, meant that security issues were not entirely new to ASEAN discussions. Security matters took on much more prominence in the Declaration issued at the 1992 Leader's Summit in Singapore, which recorded the decision to use existing mechanisms like the ASEAN-PMC to enhance dialogue on political and security matters to promote peace and stability in the region.

Planning the substance and structure of the Forum required two important exercises. The first was to determine its objectives, methodology, intellectual input and number of participants. The second was to decide on the style in which ARF meetings should be conducted.

That has been the main work undertaken since the first meeting. The Forum is now in a position to consider how those tasks are to be undertaken. Discussions on the goals and expectations of the ARF over the last two years have tended to reflect some of the following:

(a) Views converged on the need to find a means for consultations on regional political and security issues that would foster a habit of open dialogue, even when views differed on some issues, and that would encourage patterns of behaviour to reduce security risks. (Singapore, 20-21 May 1993);

(b) In a Joint Communique issued at the ASEAN Ministerial Meeting, in Bangkok, 22-23 July 1994, the Foreign Ministers noted and welcomed ASEAN's increasingly central role in fostering political and security cooperation in South-East Asia and the Asia-Pacific region, through initiatives such as the inaugural meeting of the ARF (Bangkok, 25 July 1994). They felt that the ARF could become an effective consultative Asia-Pacific forum for promoting open dialogue on political and security cooperation in the region. They considered that ASEAN should work together with the ARF to bring about a more predictable and constructive pattern of relations in the Asia-Pacific region.

(c) The ARF should ensure and preserve the current environment of peace, prosperity and cooperation in South-East Asia and the Asia-Pacific region and keep the major powers constructively engaged there, notwithstanding the changes which have taken place since the end of the cold war;

(d) The ARF should adopt comprehensive approaches to security, taking into account not only military issues, but also political, economic, social and other challenges in the region.

In evaluating those observations, the original intention of ASEAN members was that the ARF should offer regional countries and other interested parties a multilateral forum where they could consult on regional political and security matters. Though, that the ARF was established primarily to assist the cause of regional peace and stability so that economic growth could proceed. It was hoped that the process would encourage the idea of regular consultation as an important security aspect in the region.

In implementing the decision of the 1992 Summit to intensify internal dialogue on political and security matters by using the ASEAN-PMC, ASEAN envisaged a future "community of security interests in the region in which a culture of peace" would be fostered. For that reason, I believe it is essential to encourage all regional States and others directly concerned to do their part in realizing that vision. It is important for ASEAN member countries to apply the concept of "open dialogue" and to continue working creatively with ARF participants and other regional States to design a pattern of relationship in the Asia-Pacific region.

Based on the ASEAN experience, the ARF planners feel that its present Chairman must, as a first priority, concentrate on bringing all ARF members together to engage in a constructive dialogue on regional security. The first step in the process should be for people to talk to each other frankly with a view to promoting understanding. That will most probably last for a number of years to allow participants to become fully acquainted and confident with each other before moving on to more formal undertakings. ASEAN's evolution in that manner has taken almost three decades.

With ASEAN experience as a guide, the Forum, through discussion and consultation, will be able to create an atmosphere of openness and goodwill conducive to confidence-building, consensus and cooperation. The task is not simple. Flexibility and accommodation may, in the beginning, compromise the substance. In the immediate stages, while the opportunity to resolve problems can never be ruled out, it is not anticipated that dialogue and consultation will lead necessarily to the resolution of major concerns. Rather, such discussion may act as a form of moral suasion for members not to create problems among themselves. Elements of preventive diplomacy are inherent in the process. The Forum may also serve as a warning system for potential issues or problems.

The ARF's chances of success appear to be good. That optimistic view stems mainly from the special momentum created following the cold war. The Asia-Pacific region can make its contribution to the new "United Nations thinking", especially in the resolution and prevention of conflict through peaceful means and its encouragement of global efforts by regional organizations to maintain international peace and security. ASEAN has established itself as a "community of security interests" through the application of quiet diplomacy to prevent numerous inter-state conflicts. Much has already been done in the area of preventive diplomacy and CBMs in the South-East Asian region. According to some analysts, the promotion of ASEAN's ideas or strategic development of the region, such as ZOPFAN (zone of peace, freedom and neutrality) and Treaty of Amity and Cooperation and SEANFZ (Southeast Asia nuclear-weapon-free zone), are based on efforts to counter cold war tensions and confrontations. As a small group, ASEAN has no major difficulty in starting some "new thinking" for the region.

Initiatives by any of the major Powers in the region could be received with suspicion.

During the ARF-Senior Officials Meeting (SOM) and the first meeting of the Forum itself last year, many proposals were put forward. A large quantity were military-or defence-related. Many came from the developed countries and reflected the traditional western approach to security, i.e., rapid movement to transparency measures in sensitive areas. Various proposals reflected the specific security concerns of participants. Their immediate implementation should not necessarily serve as a benchmark of progress made at the Forum. The proposals submitted could be grouped in five main areas: confidence-building measures, preventive diplomacy, disarmament measures, peace-keeping and maritime issues. Rather than being classified in baskets in the western sense, proposals under the aegis of the ARF might be arranged in terms of stages, ranging from consensus-building and CBMs to preventive diplomacy measures. Their implementation will correspond closely to those stages.

While the military and defence-related aspect of security is certainly important, the ARF views security holistically, seeing the military and defense-related component as part of a comprehensive concept. Therefore, proposals brought forward during the Kathmandu meeting will be included among the ARF's matters.

# 9
# Towards A New Regional Order

After the collapse of USSR, cold war come to a virtual end. Thus many strategic changes took place in the world order. In fact, the wave of liberalisation, privatisation and globalisation is mainly responsible for bringing this dramatic change and old notions of first, second and the third world also changed.

However, United States of America took hold of being only superpower resulting in unipolarity. But many so called nations caught the vein and made tremendous success in the field of economic and strategic development. China and India are the two countries who have also a say in world affairs of present day.

India, Pakistan and Korea developed nuclear capability for military purposes. In the field of arms production and missiles they have excelled the so-called powerful nations. As such, these type of developments have brought new equations in the field of diplomatic and strategic relations. Despite burning its hands in VietNam, later and recently in Afghanistan and Iraq, the US foreign policy is still dangerous to world peace. It may interfere in regional and internal matters of nation-states. No doubt public opinion in the USA is gradually opposing this hostile and aggressive attitude of their leadership.

In the present chapter we will elucidate efforts for new stability in the east, southeast Asia and pacific region, which took its course after ninetees of the last century. No doubt a good change has come, we may await a new dawn.

The Asia-Pacific region is more peaceful now, at the beginning of the 1990s, than at any other time since 1945. There are no great-Power tensions; there are no dangerous flash-points and there are only a few relatively minor territorial disputes. The war in Cambodia is close to settlement. The Korean peninsula is relatively quiet.

The Asia-Pacific region is, however, undergoing enormous changes. It is one of the most dynamic regions in the world. The economic and technological achievements of many countries in the region are the envy of the rest of the world. But economic development—sometimes because it is lacking and sometimes because it is too uneven—has generated considerable domestic social and political flux with consequences for external strategic priorities. The most dramatic example of this may be seen in the case of China. Its domestic turmoil has affected the conduct of Chinese foreign policy and regional perceptions of China's strategic reliability.

In fact, the strategic, economic, financial, technological and historical interests of China, the United States of America, the Union of Soviet Socialist Republics and Japan interweave and overlap in the Asia-Pacific region but today do not directly conflict. India, a South Asian Power, is showing increased interest in South-East Asia but has no substantive relationships. The nuclear Powers have bilateral security relations with several of the countries of the Asia-Pacific region. The USSR has security treaties with the Democratic People's Republic of Korea and Viet Nam. China has a security treaty with the Democratic People's Republic of Korea and an "understanding" with Thailand. The United States has security ties with the Republic of Korea, Japan, Thailand, the Philippines and Australia and tacit agreements with Taiwan and with

China. The United Kingdom of Great Britain and Northern Ireland retains a connection with Hong Kong. Australia has defence co-operation agreements with Malaysia and Singapore, with New Zealand and with several of the small South Pacific island States.

As such the security element in most of these relationships is being increasingly overshadowed by the process of economic and social change and the pattern of regional economic integration. Tension and suspicion generated directly or indirectly by super-Power confrontation have been replaced by greater understanding, co-operation and an appreciation of the importance of, and mutual benefit to be derived from, trade, investment and the exchange of technology and information. Former enemies have become friends and allies.

Now, Governments and societies are more resilient, affluent and confident in their handling of intercommunal, religious and economic issues. Defence expenditure is under downward pressure in the USSR, the United States, China, the Democratic People's Republic of Korea, the Republic of Korea, Taiwan and Viet Nam. There is strong pressure for political and economic reform in the Communist States. They share a common desire to join the region-wide trend towards greater economic co-operation and commercial consultation amongst the trading nations of the Pacific rim. There are outcrops of resistance to these positive currents in the Philippines, Myanmar and the Republic of Korea and there are deep systemic and infrastructural problems in the way of progress in China, Russia and Viet Nam. And there are strains on national unity and social stability in many of the small South Pacific island countries.

On the whole, however, change in the Asia-Pacific region has contributed to a less-threatening regional security environment. As well, any security assessment of the Asia-Pacific region must take account of the uncertainties arising from leadership and generational change. Dramatically, in the Soviet Union the Communist Party was swept by such strong winds of political and economic reform unleashed by Mikhail Gorbachev that the stability of the Communist Party and the tenure of Gorbachev himself for more than one or two years could not be guaranteed. In China an aging conservative leadership has apparently lost its direction and faces a legitimacy crisis of major proportions. The leadership of the Democratic People's Republic of Korea was also at a crossroads and the outcome of the leadership succession to Kim Ilsung would have important security implications for the Republic of Korea and countries with strategic interests in north-east Asia.

Similarly, leadership in Taiwan and in the Republic of Korea can point to remarkable economic progress but both face the problem of satisfying demands for more political freedom. This could have serious consequences in Taipei because it raises the sensitive issue of Taiwanese independence. In the Philippines, Mrs. Aquino's hold on power continues to look tenuous; many issues, including the future of the United States bases and hence the existing regional security framework, could be affected if she were overthrown. Generational change elsewhere in South-East Asia seems less uncertain with preparations for the succession to Prime Minister Lee Kuan Yew in Singapore and President Suharto in Indonesia well in hand. Prime Minister Mahathir seems to have consolidated his position in Malaysia after his recent troubles. In Japan Prime Minister Toshiki Kaifu and the Liberal-Democratic Party seem to have regained control of political affairs after a year of scandal and leadership resignations.

No doubt, leadership instability in the South Pacific island States is likely to continue and, while marginal to the primary security interests of most countries in the Asia-Pacific region, it will be closely monitored by such countries as Australia, New Zealand, France, Papua New Guinea and Indonesia. India has an interest in the welfare of the

Indian community in Fiji but is too distant from the South Pacific for any significant security role.

The Russia still figures prominently in the threat analysis of defence planners in Tokyo, Beijing and Washington. From bases in the Soviet Far East, the Soviet Union can threaten Japan, China, most of America, most Pacific sea-lines of communication, much of South-East Asia and United States bases in Guam, Hawaii, the Philippines and Australia. The Soviet Union also seeks to maintain sufficient nuclear and conventional forces in the Soviet Far East to deter China from taking advantage of Soviet involvement elsewhere. The most likely threat for Japan is perceived to come from the Soviet Union with China a possibility—if it can successfully modernize—in the mid-twenty-first century. Japan's security is tied to the United States, with the not insubstantial Japanese Self-Defence Forces providing a shield to the sword of the American carrier forces. China too has long feared the Soviet Union. Over the last decade, however, through its modest but credible nuclear capability, great-Power diplomacy and large conventional forces, China has reached a point where it feels secure from the likelihood of attack from the Soviet Union and indeed from any other major Power.

No exaggeration, the United States has its most powerful military force outside the continental United States forward-deployed in the Pacific. In a global war scenario, United States maritime strategy aims to protect Western Europe, Japan and the Republic of Korea by eliminating or at least threatening to eliminate the Russia and more recently China as a Pacific Power with early offensive operations against Soviet forces and infrastructure in the Soviet Far East, particularly the Soviet Union's fleet of nuclear-powered ballistic submarines (SSBNs). Their survival is essential for the credibility of the Russian strategic nuclear retaliatory capability. For Washington, the success of the strategy depends on the correlation of a number of factors, including

Japanese military support, United States naval and nuclear access on a neither-confirm-nor-deny basis to facilities throughout the Western Pacific and perhaps, in due course, China's naval modernization.

Such a strategy is still important for Japan, the Republic of Korea, Taiwan, China, the ASEAN countries and Australia. It is, however, a less pressing priority with the current mood of relaxation, trade and dialogue in the Pacific community. If the United States forward strategy is becoming obsolete it is because, to all intents and purposes, the contest between centrally planned communism and Western democratic capitalism has been won by the West. The events unfolding in Eastern Europe and the phenomenal economic performance of many of the newly industrializing Pacific countries are testimony in this regard. Socialism as an economic model has lost its appeal. Countries in the Asia-Pacific region do not look to Moscow or Beijing; their inclination is rather to learn from Japan and the other newly industrializing market economies of east Asia. The end of bipolar confrontation between the superpowers has reduced the general level of tension in the Asia-Pacific region. The Soviet Union is less worried about NATO and China than it is about its inability to produce consumer goods and curb unrest in the Baltic States and amongst its ethnic minorities. The Sino-Soviet border is now the scene of rapidly expanding barter trade and Sino-Soviet economic co-operation on a scale unprecedented since the 1950s. China is relaxed about both the United States presence in the Western Pacific and the Soviet presence in Viet Nam.

The removal of a sense of threat on China's northern borders has reverberated southwards to the Sino-Vietnamese border—where cross-border trade has also resumed—and to Cambodia. China does not expect to be attacked by the Soviet Union. Indeed, the Gorbachev-Deng summit in May 1989 and Sino-Western disenchantment after the events in Tiananmen Square have temporarily strengthened the

Sino-Soviet relationship. Viet Nam for its part does not expect to be attacked by China again, at least in the next decade or so, except perhaps in the Spratly Islands in the South China Sea.

Taiwan is reducing its defence expenditure and does not expect to be attacked by Chinese mainland forces. The Republic of Korea and the Democratic People's Republic of Korea still fear a surprise attack each from the other but much of the heat has gone out of that once unremittingly hostile relationship. These trends have been conducive to peace in the Pacific region although as far as the big Powers are concerned, they may also have less promising long-term security implications. In general, however, the concerns of countries in the region are problems of economic growth, trade rivalries, protectionism, market access, resource diplomacy, trading blocs, technology competition, economic readjustment and the demands of a rising middle class seeking more political freedom. Few countries have a perception that they are about to be attacked or invaded by a country inside or outside the region. There seems little doubt—even in the Democratic People's Republic of Korea—that the strongest political current in the Asia-Pacific region is towards a progressive lessening of ideological differences and greater economic interdependence and co-operation. Security is less about orders of battle and more about technology and trade. Economic development has become the fundamental goal of all countries in the Asia-Pacific region. Those countries that do perform best have—among other attributes—a global marketing mentality. They are not burdened by heavy defence expenditure and, instead, spend their resources on education and technological research and development.

No doubt, Japan is universally recognized and admired as a successful economic Power, with the investment capital and technology that most countries want. Its emergence as a great Power is one of the most important strategic developments in the Asia-Pacific region. Japan, however, is entering a new phase of political influence and industrial maturity. With its accumulated wealth, diplomatic prestige and the transformation of its economy towards a high-technology structure, Japan has less need for Soviet resources and American protection. Japan's rise to great economic power has led to a relative decline in the regional importance of the United States.

The Japan-United States relationship none the less remains among the most important in the world. Defence relations have in fact been strengthened although there have been tensions over trade competition and the sharing of technology. If the United States continues to press Japan to increase substantially its military budget and play a larger security role in east Asia, other regional countries will be disconcerted. They prefer a Japan that does not shift away from the reassuring predictability that is, they perceive, provided by Japan's subordinate security relationship with the United States.

China and the Russia retain a residual core of distrust about Japan but on the whole they seem to have moved towards the ASEAN position, that is, acceptance of Japan's right to have a modest military force and acknowledgement of Japan's status as a wealthy banker and investor, as a leader in advanced technologies and as the world's largest giver of aid.

In fact, Japan's primary concern is the maintenance of its economic prosperity. Japan's sense of comprehensive national security goes beyond narrow concepts of military security. It is using methods similar to those applied by the United States in Europe after 1945. Japan is expanding its regional aid and investment programme throughout the Asia-Pacific region from China in the north to the island countries of the South Pacific in a burden-sharing approach that complements the United States military contribution. Japan has, for example, offered to fund the cost of a political settlement and peace-keeping operations in Cambodia. It is likely to use its economic influence in Manila to encourage the Philippines to continue hosting the United States bases. It supports efforts to create an OECD-type of arrangement in the Pacific through the Pacific Economic Co-operation Community and the Asia-Pacific Economic Forum. Perhaps the greatest uncertainty in the Asia-Pacific region has been presented by the crisis in China. China is still emerging as a major actor in the Pacific region in a variety of roles. Optimistic expectations about China's ability to become a modernized State and a responsible member of the Asia-Pacific community were thrown into doubt by developments in Beijing in June 1989. The killings in Tiananmen Square precipitated a profound crisis of confidence in Hong Kong with the political effects rippling throughout the region.

Many Western analysts believe China's hopes for modernization have been set back by several years. Others are even more pessimistic. If China's reform processes remain stymied by a conservative central leadership, persistent economic problems could stoke social and political unrest well into the 1990s. On the other hand, a too rapid decentralization of political and economic control would have equally disastrous consequences. It was not long, moreover, before Hong Kong's stock market recovered all the ground lost in June 1989. Although there will continue to be lingering suspicion about China's domestic agenda and the ability of the Chinese Communist Party to govern a capitalist enclave such as Hong Kong in the lead up to 1997, it seems likely that Hong Kong will survive the many pessimistic assessments currently floating around.

This is provided, of course, that a satisfactory formula balancing the authoritarian nature of the Chinese Communist Party and the social, economic and political demands of the Chinese people can be achieved in the next one or two years. Equally important for regional security will be the outcome of reform in other Communist States, particularly the Democratic People's Republic of Korea. The Republic of Korea's economic indicators show impressive economic gains. Together with the Republic of Korea's growing military strength, these have compounded the problems of the Democratic People's Republic of Korea. Pyongyang's political, social and economic system and its foreign policy approach are unique but outmoded.

The Democratic People's Republic of Korea suffers from all the disadvantages of an autarkic central command economy. Productivity and per capita income are one fifth of that in the Republic of Korea. Most consumer goods are in scarce supply. Many factories are simply obsolescent.

Foreign exchange is lacking; international debts cannot be paid and there is little foreign investment. Tension in the Korean peninsula has none the less declined sharply in the last few years, primarily because of the rapid improvement in relations between China, the USSR and the United States. This has forced the Democratic People's Republic of Korea to re-examine its policies towards Seoul and to contemplate some, albeit cautious, domestic political and economic reforms of its own.

In fact, South-East Asia no country is threatened with direct aggression by any other country. Thailand is not threatened by Viet Nam, now chastened and impoverished and, until its withdrawal from Cambodia, a regional pariah. Thailand in fact is regarded as a candidate for status as one of the newly industrializing economies of Asia; it has security guarantees from both China and the United States and has been a beneficiary of the war in Cambodia. Singapore has a sense of vulnerability owing to its position as a small rich Chinese island State surrounded by the large States of Malaysia and Indonesia. Singapore has made much of threats to ASEAN by the Soviet Union and Viet Nam, partly in order to focus ASEAN attention on an external threat. Singapore wants to preserve a United

States military presence in the Philippines or, if necessary, in Singapore.

The Philippines has been preoccupied with problems of income inequality, poverty, underdevelopment, deteriorating terms of trade, a heavy external debt and accompanying domestic insurgencies and leadership instability. Manila's external security interests have been protected by the United States. The substantial United States military presence in the Philippines has, however, contributed directly to the internal social and political problems of the Philippines.

Neither Malaysia nor Indonesia perceives a direct or immediate threat to its security. Both find themselves in a relatively secure environment. Both have developed close bilateral military ties and hold regular joint exercises for their three armed services. Malaysian and Indonesian concerns are with the coherence and unity of ASEAN policies, the activities of foreign navies and regional trading blocs, a resolution of the Cambodia war and such regional issues as the security problems in Irian Jaya and in East Timor, but these are not of compelling national importance. Indonesia has worked hard to establish a considerably improved relationship with Australia and Papua New Guinea. An area of diminishing concern is the war in Cambodia. That war is almost over as far as Thailand's Prime Minister Chatichai Choonhavan is concerned. He wants Thailand to take advantage of the commercial opportunities in Indochina ahead of competitors from Taiwan, Hong Kong and the Republic of Korea. Viet Nam's conflict with China has eased and it seems poised to break out of its isolation in the region since the completion of its troop withdrawals in September 1989.

The war inside Cambodia may continue at a low level, but provided that the Hun Sen Government can survive the present onslaught by the Khmer Rouge and their non-Communist allies, it will probably be accorded diplomatic recognition with the passage of time. Several European countries and the European Parliament have manifested an inclination to accept the reality of the Hun Sen Government in Phnom Penh and cut their support for the fiction that a fractious Thailand-based coalition led by the Khmer Rouge can in any way represent the Government of Cambodia.

They are also embarrassed by the Khmer Rouge, whose dismal human rights record has been compared with that of the Nazis of the Second World War. Cambodia, in other words, is no longer the dominant security issue for countries in South-East Asia that it once was.

ASEAN was formed in 1967 largely because of security considerations. Much of what held it together in the 1970s and 1980s came from the concern of member countries about the situation in Cambodia and the perception of a threat from Viet Nam. These concerns have now largely dissipated. There is a question whether in the future there will be challenges as serious as the Cambodian issue that will be sufficient to transcend ASEAN racial, cultural, political and economic differences. The ASEAN countries no longer perceive a threat from China or from any other external Power. Indonesia is proceeding towards a resumption of diplomatic relations with China although there is still suspicion of Chinese regional ambitions and fear about renewed contact between Beijing and the several hundred thousand overseas Chinese resident in Indonesia.

Each ASEAN country has its own internal political and foreign policy agenda, and ambitions. There is limited intra-regional trade and most of the ASEAN countries have trade links outside ASEAN. There is no ASEAN defence co-operation as such: the Philippines and Thailand have defence arrangements with the United States and/or China. Singapore and Malaysia are members of the Five Power Defence Arrangement with the United Kingdom, Australia and New Zealand. There are other anomalies. Thailand's close relations with China are looked at askance by Indonesia;

Singapore and Indonesia have different attitudes on ASEAN's approach to Viet Nam; and Malaysia and Indonesia have objected to Singapore's unilateral offer to host United States military facilities.

However, the ASEAN States have become accustomed to the operational structure of ASEAN as a regional forum. They have enjoyed the prestige and influence of their collective membership in ASEAN in the wider regional and global context. ASEAN is a successful formula. Moreover, the ASEAN States share a common interest in balancing the presence and pressures of the big outside Powers and, as a regional group of developing non-Communist economies, they have a common interest in challenging Japan, the European Community and the United States. They have many different points of view but nevertheless the ASEAN States will be forced to combine their economic bargaining power as much as possible if they hope to deal effectively with the rest of the world. If ASEAN is joined by other South-East Asian countries, it will be an even stronger regional economic and political group. The solidarity of ASEAN on agricultural protectionism and at the recent Asia-Pacific Economic Forum in Canberra are instances of the way this new co-operation is already working.

The fact that super-Power tension has eased has led many countries in the Asia-Pacific region to argue for more, not less, defence expenditure. They want more modern defence technology and equipment on the grounds that the withdrawal of the super-Powers from more direct military competition in the Asia-Pacific region leaves the way open for regional Powers to vie for influence in the ensuing vacuum. This kind of assessment has reinforced tendencies for regional military build-up as countries in the region follow the lead of neighbouring States. Chinese military forces on the Spratly Islands are effectively stationed in the very centre of the South-East Asian land/sea environment. The numbers involved are small but they are perceived as representing a bridgehead for China's plans to consolidate its claims in the South China Sea and build up its presence in South-East Asia.

Indian strategists cite China's naval expansion into the South China Sea as one of the key reasons for the development of Indian naval facilities in the Andaman and Nicobar islands at the western entrance to the Malacca Strait. Japan, meanwhile, is a major military Power. Despite the relatively low percentage of its GNP spent on defence, the amount is increasing in real terms to the point where Japan has the third highest defence expenditure in the world and the world's fifth largest navy. The amount spent on defence is to be increased by 6 per cent in the coming year. Japan has a force structure suitable for rapid expansion and it clearly could support much larger and longer-range armed forces than it does today.

There has been some discussion in Japan of defensive aircraft carriers that could be used to protect Japanese sea-lines of communication. Singapore has expressed regional concerns about these trends by its recent offer to host some of the American facilities currently located in the Philippines. Singapore fears that other great Powers as well as perhaps Japan would feel obliged or tempted to fill the gap left by the United States. Malaysia and Indonesia have expressed concern about the ability of China to project naval power into the South China Sea.

They are also concerned about India's naval expansion and the development of its ability to project tridimensional naval forces in a maritime are that stretches from the west coast of the Horn of Africa to the Andaman and Nicobar Islands adjacent to South-East Asia. Malay sian officials have suggested that Kuala Lumpur could follow the Thai example and lean towards China in the face of any substantially increased Indian naval activity in South-East Asia.

Economically, it is forecast that the Asia-Pacific region has expanded more rapidly than most other parts of the world. The newly industrializing economies of Asia are growing fast. They see new market and investment opportunities in the reformist Communist economies. The insurgencies which once plagued many countries in South-East Asia have been eclipsed by the problems of rapid economic growth. Chin Peng, former Secretary-General of the Communist Party of Malaya, is the most recent Communist in South-East Asia to publicly renounce armed struggle in favour of the parliamentary road to socialism. Assured of domestic political and social stability and, in relative terms, with more money to spend, the nations of Asia are expanding their military capabilities. In particular, as they exercise their national sovereignty over offshore resources delineated by the International Convention on the Law of the Sea, they are putting more effort into acquiring high-technology air and maritime forces.

A regional naval build-up could gain momentum from developments in the Philippines, currently host country to the biggest forward-based American military presence in the Pacific. Those developments are designed to support United States military operations in the Western Pacific, north-east Asia, the Indian Ocean and the Persian Gulf. The bases help preserve the strategic balance in the Asia-Pacific region. The agreement concerning the bases expires in September 1991. A continued United States military presence in the Philippines is considered to be of major importance to the security of the United States, Japan, Singapore, Thailand, Australia and New Zealand.

But several ASEAN States, particularly Indonesia, do not perceive the prospective loss of the United States bases as catastrophic for regional security. They even suggest that a United States withdrawal could be followed by a Soviet pull-out and thereby improve the chances for ASEAN to achieve its goal of a South-East Asian zone of peace, freedom and neutrality (ZOPFAN). Some would argue that the removal of the bases at a time of their decreasing strategic importance would contribute to greater stability in the Philippines and hence to greater regional security.

As well as opposition to the American presence in the Philippines, there is an expectation of a reduced United States naval and military presence in the Western Pacific in the face of domestic United States constraints on defence expenditure, growing nationalism in Japan and the Republic of Korea and the decline in Soviet naval deployments in the Pacific. On the other hand, many countries fear that a declining United States presence will contribute to a competition for influence by other ascending great Powers, such as India, China, Japan and perhaps Indonesia.

Developments in the island countries of the South Pacific are, although relatively volatile, of little direct security concern to countries in the Asia-Pacific region apart from Australia, New Zealand and Indonesia. The suddenly volatile politics of the South Pacific were nowhere more apparent than in the coups in Fiji in 1987 and signs of a disregard for law and order and constitutional government in Papua New Guinea, Vanuatu and Palau.

The general prospect is for continued uncertainty and the constant fear of intervention by outside influences. The solution lies in economic development and increased foreign aid. Australia is playing a more active role and has increased its defence ties in the region. France and the United States have tried to improve their respective regional images, with some success. Japan has shown an increasing interest in bolstering the Western presence in the South Pacific with economic aid and investment. The ASEAN States, led by Indonesia, also seek to contribute to stability in the South Pacific by developing closer political relations with Pacific island States, particularly Papua New Guinea and Fiji.

For Western Powers, such as the United States and Australia, earlier concerns about an intrusive Soviet presence have now eased with the retreat of Soviet naval activities to the North Pacific and the positive impact of Gorbachev's Pacific diplomacy since his 1986 speech at Vladivostock. United States concern about New Zealand's anti-nuclear policy and the implications of the Treaty of Rarotonga, which established the South Pacific Nuclear-Free Zone, is now much reduced as neither development has proved significant as far as United States naval activities in the Pacific are concerned.

As such, throughout the Asia-Pacific region there is general concern about the proliferation of chemical weapons and the spread of nuclear weapons and ballistic-missile technology. Ballistic-missile technology is more and more freely available. Several States in east Asia and south Asia have a short-range ballistic-missile capability. These systems, armed with conventional warheads or, more disturbing, equipped with chemical weapons or nuclear weapons, could upset existing regional balances. They could contribute to regional arms races that would be difficult to control because of problems of verification, especially with regard to chemical weapons.

The Democratic People's Republic of Korea is building a nuclear weapons research capability according to American intelligence reports based on satellite photographs of a nuclear reactor, a plutonium extraction plant and other facilities in the Democratic People's Republic of Korea. Fears have been expressed about the consequences of a possible nuclear arms race in south Asia.

Another regional concern is the proliferation of weapons producers and competition for arms sales from a range of countries. But generally the security outlook for the Asia-Pacific region at the beginning of the 1990s would have to be described as reasonably good. Threat assessments are, frequently, vaguely defined forecasts which, while acknowledging the current optimism, also warn of unforeseeable threats arising in the future from rapid social and economic change and great-Power re-alignments. For individual countries the outlook is generally favourable, with a few exceptions, including China, the Philippines, Myanmar and the Democratic People's Republic of Korea. Their problems are not problems of military security as such. They are, rather, problems of poverty and the struggle for economic development.

# 10
# Koreas on Regional Security

## I

## DEMOCRATIC PEOPLE'S REPUBLIC OF KOREA

No doubt, a unipolar world emerged with the dissolution of the former Soviet Union and the end of the cold war, and one military bloc became dominant. The Warsaw Pact ceased to exist, while the North Atlantic Treaty Organization (NATO) has intensified its róle. The process of confidence-building, security and disarmament in Europe was thrown off balance, giving way to intra-national and ethnic conflicts. This is clear proof that nowhere on the planet is there an exemplary regime for confidence-building and security.

### Peace, Security and Disarmament in the Asia-Pacific Region

It is significant to note that the Asia-Pacific region, still burdened with the legacy of the cold war, constitutes a threat to international peace, security and disarmament, owing to the actions of certain States poised to fill the power vacuum created in the post-cold war period. As the economy of the Asia-Pacific region has developed rapidly and its strategic importance has been recognized, powerful countries, supported by their own military strength, have been pursuing policies of domination and hegemony there. A such military confrontation and the intensification of arms races between countries of the Asia-Pacific region. Another reason for the lack of peace, security and disarmament is the continuation of unjustifiable political and military pressure and threats.

Basically, each country pursues its own interests rather than trying to solve conflicts with its neighbours in a mutually beneficial way. The current situation proves that it is possible to promote regional disarmament and security only after bilateral confidence has been established. As long as one nation is afraid of being victimized by another, confidence cannot be established and, peace, security and disarmament cannot be realized.

It must be remembered that confidence-building starts with dialogue and negotiation, a process that the present situation on the Korean peninsula clearly calls for.

**Current Situation in the DPRK**

Today our people are grieving deeply over the unexpected passing, in July 1994, of the Great Leader, Comrade Kim Il Sung, whom they hold in higher esteem than any other figure in the 5,000-year history of the nation. They grieve for the loss of their fatherly Leader, who devoted his life to their freedom and liberation, to the prosperity and development of the country and to world peace. We firmly believe that our respected and beloved Leader will always be with us.

Our people could not have transformed their loss into strength and courage had it not been for another Great Leader, Comrade Kim Jong Il, who has been wisely directing the general work of the party. State and army for some time.

Things are going well in the DPRK because the Dear Leader Comrade Kim Jong Il is inheriting what the Great Leader worked for during his lifetime.

## Confidence-Building: The Key to Peace, Security and Disarmament

### *The DPRK-United States Agreed Framework*

Implementation of the DPRK-United States Agreed Framework is the means at present for establishing confidence and paving the way for peace, security and disarmament on the Korean peninsula.

On 16 June 1994, shortly before his death. Comrade Kim II Sung met with former United States President Jimmy Carter, who was on a visit to the DPRK, and clarified our position, that the nuclear issue could be resolved through dialogue and negotiations between the DPRK and the United States; confidence-building between both countries was the main approach.

Our Government, honouring the will of the Great Leader, concluded the DPRK-United States talks, which had lasted about a year and half, by adopting the historic DPRK-United States Agreed Framework in October 1994. The adoption is of great significance for giving impetus to peace and reunification of the Korean peninsula and to building peace and security in Asia and the world. The Agreed Framework is an historic document, guaranteed by the two Heads of State, and marks a turning-point in the resolution of the nuclear issue on the Korean peninsula and in the development of the DPRK-United States relations.

If the Agreed Framework is implemented, hostile relations between the two countries will come to an end, finally leading the way towards confidence, a full resolution of the nuclear issue on the Korean peninsula, and the denuclearization of that area.

The DPRK Government is making every sincere effort to implement the Agreed Framework. Some forces, however, are spreading rumours which could have a negative impact on implementation and are an attempt to aggravate the situation on the Korean peninsula and to disturb the smooth implementation of the Agreed Framework, which has entered a new stage. Implementation must be encouraged rather than complicated if the nuclear issue here is to be resolved.

### *A New Peace Agreement*

A new peace agreement between the DPRK and the United States would be the principal means of building confidence and defusing tension. It would replace the Korean Armistice Agreement. The Korean peninsula urgently requires legally binding assurances for solid peace.

The Armistice Agreement, as the name implies, is an agreement to enforce a temporary cease-fire, and its implementation mechanism is a supervisory body. The Government of the DPRK proposed 20 years ago that the Armistice Agreement be replaced with a peace agreement, and in April 1994 it renewed that proposal.

The work to build a framework for peace and security on the Korean peninsula through negotiation is already under way with the withdrawal of the Korea-China representation—one side of the signatories of the Military Armistice Commission—and the opening of the representative office of the Korean People's Army, in Panmunjom.

If the new peace arrangement is established, peace and security in this region will be legally assured, since the North and South confirmed their commitment to non-aggression in 1991 Agreement on Reconciliation, Non-Aggression, and Cooperation and Exchange between the North and South.

### *Reunification*

Reunification of the country is the cornerstone for building confidence, peace, security and disarmament on the Korean peninsula. Last year. President Kim II Sung took steps that opened up a new phase in efforts towards reunification. The tireless efforts of the respected Leader were geared to the reunification of the motherland and to transforming confrontation into dialogue and negotiation.

Those efforts filled the nation with hopes for reunification. The South Korean authorities, however, took action against the nation and reunification by pointing their weapons at the hearts of their fellow countrymen and taking the road towards a fascist crack-down during the period of mourning for the Great Leader, instead of expressing their condolences as a partner in the reunification dialogue and as a part of the Korean nation.

The policies of our Government are consistent. We maintain the principles of independent and peaceful reunification in great national unity, as set forth by the Great Leader during his lifetime.

The 'Ten-Point Programme of Great Unity of the Whole Nation for the Reunification of the Country", advanced by the Great Leader in April 1993, constituted a guideline for putting an end to 50 years of division and confrontation. It stipulates that a unified State should be established which would represent all political parties, social organizations and individuals from all walks of life, and would leave intact the existing two systems and two Governments. Furthermore, it is made clear that the unified State—a confederal Government equally represented by the regional Governments of the North and South—should be an independent, peaceful and non-aligned neutral State.

If the pan-national State based on confederation is established, security issues on the Korean peninsula, such as denuclearization and disarmament, will be resolved as a matter of course. Development of a North-South dialogue would be one of the essential elements in achieving reunification. The main obstacles to the opening of humanitarian exchanges, dialogue and contacts are the existence of the "National Security Law" of South Korea, which labels the members of the same nation as an "enemy", and the concrete walls, symbols of division and confrontation. Therefore, all legal and physical barriers should be removed as soon as" possible in order to achieve free contacts, exchange and cooperation between the North and South and to bring about great national unity.

## ANNEX

### Ten-Point Programme on the Great Unity of the Whole Nation for the Reunification of the Country

To put an end to the nearly half a century of division and confrontation and reunify the country is the unanimous demand and desire of the whole nation. For the independent and peaceful reunification of the country it is necessary to achieve the great unity of the whole nation. All those who are concerned about the destiny of the nation—whether they be in the North, or in the South, or overseas, and whether they be communists, or nationalists, rich, or poor, artists, or believers—must unite as one nation, transcending all their differences, and together pave the way for national reunification.

Those with strength devoting their strength, those with knowledge giving their knowledge and those with money donating their money, all should make a tangible contribution to the reunification of the country and development and prosperity of a reunified land, thus putting an end to national division and displaying the dignity and honour of the reunited 70 million fellow countrymen to the world.

1. A unified State independent, peaceful and neutral, should be founded through the unity of the whole nation.

The North and South should found a pan-national unified State to represent all parties, all groups and all the members of the nation from all walks of life, while leaving the existing two systems and two governments intact. The pan-national unified State should be a confederal State in which the two regional governments of the North and the South are represented equally, and an independent, peaceful and non-aligned neutral State which is not aligned with any great Power.

2. Unity should be based on patriotism and the spirit of national independence.

All the members of the nation link their individual destiny with that of the nation, love their nation passionately and unite with the single desire to defend the independence of the nation. They should display dignity and pride in being members of our nation and reject sycophancy and national nihilism that erode the nation's consciousness of independence.

3. Unity should be achieved on the principle of promoting co-existence, co-prosperity and common interests and subordinating everything to the cause of national reunification.

The North and South should recognize and respect the existence of different beliefs, ideas and systems, and achieve joint progress and prosperity, with neither side encroaching on the other. They should promote the interests of the whole nation before regional class interests and direct every effort to the accomplishment of the cause of national reunification.

4. All political disputes that foment division and confrontation between fellow countrymen should be ended and unity should be achieved.

The North and South should refrain from seeking or fomenting confrontation, end all political disputes between them and stop abusing and slandering each other. As fellow countrymen they should not be hostile to each other and, through the united efforts of the nation, they should counter foreign aggression and interference.

5. Fear of invasion from both South and North and the ideas of prevailing over communism and of communization should be dispelled, and North and South should believe in each other and unite.

The North and the South should not threaten and invade each other. Neither side should try to force its systems on the other or to absorb the other.

6. The North and South should value democracy and join hands on the road to national reunification, without rejecting each other, because of differences in ideals and principles.

They should guarantee the freedom of debate on and of activities for reunification and should not suppress, take reprisals against, persecute or punish political opponents. They should not arrest anyone because of their pro-North or pro-South tendencies and should release and reinstate all political prisoners so that they may contribute to the cause of national reunification.

7. The North and South should protect the material and spiritual wealth of individuals and organizations and encourage their use for the promotion of great national unity.

Both before reunification and after it they should recognize State ownership, co-operative ownership and private ownership and protect the capital and prosperity of individuals and organizations, as well as all interests concerned with foreign capital. They should recognize the social reputation and qualifications of individuals in all domains including science, education, literature, the arts, public debate, the press, health care and sports, and continue to guarantee the benefits granted to people who have performed meritorious services.

8. Understanding, trust and unity should be built up

across the nation through contact, exchange visits and dialogue.

All the obstacles to contact and exchange visits should be removed and the door should be opened for everyone without discrimination to undertake exchange visits. All the parties, groupings and people of all social standings should be given equal opportunities to conduct dialogue, and bilateral and multilateral dialogue should be developed.

9. The whole nation, North, South and overseas, should strengthen its solidarity for the sake of national reunification.

Things beneficial to national reunification should be supported and encouraged in an unbiased manner and things harmful to it should be rejected in the North, in the South and overseas, and all should assist and cooperate with one another, going beyond their own narrow enclosure. All political parties, organizations and the people from all walks of life in the North, in the South and overseas should be allied organizationally in the patriotic work to achieve national reunification.

10. Those who have contributed to the great unity of the nation and to the cause of national reunification should be honoured.

Special favours should be granted to those who have performed exploits for the sake of the great unity of the nation and the reunification of the country, to patriotic martyrs and to their descendants. If those who had turned their back on the nation in the past return to the patriotic road, repentant of their past, they should be dealt with leniently and assessed fairly according to the contribution they have made to the cause of national reunification.

## II

## REPUBLIC OF KOREA ON PEACE AND SECURITY

The Korean peninsula is a region where arms control and confidence-building measures are badly needed. From 1950 to 1953, Korea experienced a devastating war, and ever since then the arms race between the Republic of Korea (ROK) and the Democratic People's Republic of Korea (DPRK) has continued without any sign of easing. Currently, the peninsula is one of the few areas of acute military confrontation in the world. Along the 155-mile demarcation line dividing the South and the North, about one and a half million heavily armed soldiers confront each other (Table 1). In that situation, there is an urgent need in the peninsula for arms control on a bilateral basis. This need can be explored from four major perspectives.

### The Need for Arms Control

First, it is imperative to actualize arms control in order to establish a solid peace system and ultimately to achieve the peaceful unification of the Korean peninsula. A peace system without any military confidence-building measures or any arms reduction between the South and the North would be unstable. Since the legacy of the Korean War still remains, and intense military confrontation exists along the Demilitarized Zone, there are real dangers of renewed armed conflict. The sheer size of the forces arrayed on both sides—a million in the North and 650,000 in the South—is dangerous enough. This military concentration along the demarcation line raises the risk of an impulsive reaction in tense times. The recent downing of a United States helicopter that strayed into North Korea's airspace showed how easily shooting could begin on the Korean peninsula. In those circumstances, nothing is more important than preventing renewed conflict from occurring and establishing a solid peace structure. Arms control will prevent movement towards a South-North war and will enhance military stability.

Second, arms control is needed to release resources for economic development as a long-term strategy for the prosperity of the Korean peninsula. The division of the peninsula and the continued arms race between the two Koreas have brought about a serious security dilemma whereby the more defensive measures one party adopts to increase its sense of security, the more insecure the other party feels. The latter then takes additional measures of its own, which causes the former to take more measures, and so on. That security dilemma has not only undermined political and military stability on the Korean peninsula, but has also adversely affected economic development. There is a need to reduce the military share of the gross national product (GNP) and to enhance the economic well-being of the Korean people.

Third, arms control is needed to overcome the cold war legacy on the peninsula and to contribute to the stability of the North-East Asian region as a whole. The end of the cold war has greatly improved the security climate in the region—the immense ideological barrier that gave rise to distrust and hostility among States for decades—has collapsed. While that does not necessarily mean that peace has finally arrived, the improvements in relations between States in the region clearly provide new opportunities for the future. Military confrontation on the Korean peninsula has been a major obstacle to securing peace and stability in North-East Asia. In order to pave the way to a regional security arrangement, the question of a divided Korea needs to be settled first.

Ultimately, arms control between North and South Korea is necessary to obtain international support in the process of unifying the peninsula. If the two Koreas achieve unification without any arms control measures or arms reduction, a unified Korea will possess enormous military strength. Among the major Powers in North-East Asia, there is real concern about a *militarily-strengthened united* Korea.

No major Power wants a nuclear-armed united Korea. Since Korean unification needs to take place in the context of expanding regional cooperation in North-East Asia, it is desirable to eliminate that negative concern of its neighbours.

**Recent Security Developments**

The Korean peninsula is often described as the "last bastion or glacier of the cold war", owing to the ongoing acute military confrontation between the North and South. Over the past few years, however, there have been several major developments which have affected the security environment of the peninsula. Three events are worth noting in the exploration of the arms control possibilities between the two Koreas.

First, two important agreements were adopted in late 1991 and early 1992 that demonstrate significant progress in inter-Korean relations: the Agreement on Reconciliation, Non-Aggression, and Cooperation and Exchange between the South and the North (appropriately known as the "Basic Agreement"), and the Joint Declaration on the Denuclearization of the Korean Peninsula. Both agreements came into effect on 19 February 1992.

The Basic Agreement was the first official document governing basic inter-Korean relations that was consented to by the two Korean Governments. It covers three basic areas: political, military, and a multifaceted exchange and cooperation—overcoming sharp differences in past positions. For its part, the Joint Declaration stipulates, among other things, that both sides will not manufacture, produce, possess, or use nuclear weapons and that a joint nuclear control commission should be established, with a mandate to carry out inspections to verify that the Korean peninsula is nuclear-free. An additional important commitment is the prohibition of nuclear reprocessing and uranium enrichment facilities.

After the Basic Agreement and the Joint Declaration entered into force, various subcommittees and commissions were established, and a series of subsidiary protocols were adopted in September 1992. Implementation of the agreements and protocols has been delayed, however, by North Korea's unwillingness to develop the inter-Korean dialogue, including its reluctance to be transparent regarding its nuclear programme.

Second, there was a leadership change in North Korea in July 1994, caused by the passing of the North's founder, Kim II Sung. There has been much speculation about the future of the post-Kim II Sung North Korea. Although the future of that country, which has been almost impenetrable to outsiders, falls into the realm of speculation rather than prediction, the following assessment seems to receive broad support: North Korea will attempt changes in its economic and external policies, although the nature of change and reform which Pyongyang's new leadership is expected to undertake will be far from wide-ranging.

Third, the United States and North Korea finally adopted an Agreed Framework in Geneva in October 1994 to resolve the nuclear issue on the Korean peninsula. The primary importance of the Geneva agreement is that it provides a framework for the ultimate resolution of North Korea's nuclear issue, which has seriously threatened peace and stability on the Korean peninsula, as well as in North-East Asia, for the past two years. The Agreement was a compromise and, as such, has received mixed reviews. The centrepiece of the deal is the provision of light-water reactors to North Korea in return for the freezing and eventual dismantling of the North's graphite-moderated reactors and related facilities. Complete transparency in North Korea's nuclear activities, particularly its past activities, will not be secured until some time in the future, perhaps as late as five years from now.

Another significant feature of the Geneva Agreement is that Pyongyang has pledged to "consistently take steps" to implement the North-South Joint Declaration of the Denuclearization of the Korean Peninsula and to engage in the North-South dialogue. Pyongyang should re-engage Seoul if it expects rapid progress in implementing those aspects of the Agreement having to do with the overall normalization of relations and the supply of light-water reactors—aspects in respect to which the ROK will be a major player.

The types of arms control measures that can be introduced on the Korean peninsula are open-ended. In that regard, the Basic Agreement provides an important guideline. The Agreement, as a road map towards peaceful coexistence, requires the two Koreas to endeavour together to transform the present armistice into a solid peace. It contains specific confidence and security-building measures, as well as arms control measures, the goal of which is to end the costly arms race and confrontation between the two parts of Korea.

For instance, article 12 of the Agreement provides that the two sides shall discuss and carry out steps "to build military confidence and realize arms reductions, including the mutual notification and control of major movements of military units and major military exercises, the peaceful utilization of the Demilitarized Zone, exchanges of military personnel and information, phased reductions in armaments including the elimination of weapons of mass destruction and attack capabilities, and verifications thereof. The Agreement and the subsidiary Protocol also indicate that a telephone hot line should be installed between the military authorities of both sides to prevent accidental armed clashes and their escalation, and a joint military commission shall be established in order to discuss concrete measures to prevent military confrontation.

In addition to the basic Agreement and subsidiary Protocol, existing international arrangements and institutions could also be utilized to facilitate arms control on the Korean peninsula. Currently, various efforts to stop arms proliferation are being employed at both global and regional levels. For instance, coordinated participation in the United Nations Register of Conventional Arms, which was opened on 1 January 1992, may be useful on the Korean peninsula. The Register asks Member States to provide data from the previous calendar year on an annual basis in respect of import into and export from their territory of seven categories of major armaments.

The Register could perform such a confidence-building function if the requested data were provided within the stipulated time-frame by both the South and the North. The list of arms control measures applicable to the Korean peninsula is clearly open-ended (Annex 1). To initiate arms control, however, measures such as those listed in the annex should be implemented as soon as possible and in good faith.

On the basis of their implementation, further effective steps, namely, the control of the structure of the military forces or arms reduction, may be explored.

For effective arms reduction between the two Koreas, the following working principles and objectives need to be considered:

1. The final objective of arms reduction should be the strengthening of stability and security on the Korean peninsula through the establishment of a stable and secure balance of defensive forces at appropriately lower levels;

2. The initial phase should eliminate military disparities between the two Koreas and subsequently proceed to further mutually agreed reductions;
3. The appropriate level of military strength to be maintained in the subsequent stages should be mutually agreed. The need for self-defence as an independent unified nation should be satisfied, taking into consideration the geostrategic location of the Korean peninsula, the history of foreign intervention, and the changes in the North-East Asian region;
4. As a matter of high priority, the capability for launching a surprise attack and for initiating large-scale offensive action should be eliminated, together with the reduction of weapons of mass destruction;
5. The overall verifiable levels of offensive equipment, such as tanks, artillery and armoured personnel carriers, central to the seizing and holding of territory, must be reduced radically in the first stage of reductions;
6. The number of military personnel may be reduced in accordance with reductions in armaments and equipment;
7. The reserve forces may be reduced in parallel with the reduction of regular forces;
8. Foreign military forces may be reduced gradually and withdrawn in accordance with the progress made in structural arms control between the two Koreas;
9. Compliance with all the agreed measures of arms reduction should be verified through an effective and strict verification regime that would include, among other things, provisions for on-site inspection and the exchange of information. Appropriate sanctions should be applied in cases of non-compliance and violation of agreements;

10. Towards that end, it is desirable to form and operate an international supervisory group that includes the two Koreas.

It is obvious from the foregoing analysis that both the Koreas are deeply concerned about the peace and security in the region. In fact, though not much headway is made, it can be surmised that an amicable solution to the current imbroglio can be reached. Let us be optimistic. If the Berlin Wall can fall why not Koreas be unified.

# 11

# Malaysian Army: A Study

Though not a significant military power in the region, Malaysia is an emerging economic power. In this chapter we will give an acount of Malaysian armey.

It is pertinent to note that the first military units in Malaysia can be traced back to the Malay States Volunteer Rifles which existed from 1915 to 1936. The birth of the Malaysian Army came about when the Federal Council of Federated Malay States eventually passed the Malay Regiment Bill on 23 January 1933. This allowed the initial recruitment of 25 males for the First Experimental Malay Company on 1 March 1933. Major G. McI. S. Bruce of the Lincolnshire Regiment was the first Commanding Officer.

By 1 January 1935, the Experimental Company became The Malay Regiment with a complement of 150 men. A battalion was formed on 1 January 1938 and eventually a second battalion on 1 December 1941.

The 1st Bn Malay Regiment was famous for its defence of Opium Hill or Bukit Chandu in Singapore. The 'Battle of Opium Hill' on 14 February 1942 involved 42 soldiers commanded by Lt. Adnan Bin Saidi who defended their position against attack from the 18th Division of the Japanese Imperial Army under Lt. Gen. Renya Mutaguchi. After World War II and during the Malayan Emergency, the number of battalions was increased to 7 in the early 1950s.

The Kor Armor DiRaja (Royal Armoured Corps) can

trace its roots to the formation on 1 September 1952 of the Federation Reconnaissance Squadron. It was later merged with the Federation Regiment to form the Federation Reconnaissance Corps. The name underwent a few transformations from the Malaysian Reconnaissance Corps (16 September 1967), Royal Malaysian Reconnaissance Corps (May 1979) to Royal Cavalry Corps (December 1979) and finally to Kor Armor DiRaja (Royal Armoured Corps) on 8 December 1986.

**Organisation and Structure**

The Malaysian Army is currently organised into four Divisions and are placed under the Field Army Headquarters. Three of which (the 2nd, 3rd and 4th Divisions) are based in Peninsular Malaysia and the fourth (the 1st Division) is based in East Malaysia. The *Grup Gerak Khas* (Special Forces group), 10th Parachute Brigade and the *Pasukan Udara Tentera Darat* (army aviation) are independent formations and directly subordinate to the Chief of the Army.

Notably, the Malaysian Army currently has 17 Corps or Regiments in the organisation. These are grouped into 3 main components, the Combat Element, The Combat Support Element and the Support Elements.

**Rank Structure**

It is pertinent to note that Malaysian Army uses a rank structure inherited from the British Army which has 17 levels from Private (*Prebet*) to General (*Jeneral*). These ranks are divided into 2 groups - Officer (*Pegawai*) and Other Ranks (*Lain-Lain Pangkat*) which includes the Non-Commissioned Officer (*Pegawai Tanpa Tauliah*) ranks.

***Officers***

Officers are sub-divided into 3 groups:-

Senior Officers This group consists of officers holding

the ranks of Lieutenant Colonel (*Leftenan Kolonel*), Colonel (*Kolonel*), Brigadier General (*Brigedier Jeneral*), Major General (*Mejar Jeneral*), Lieutenant General (*Leftenan Jeneral*) and General (*Jeneral*)

***Field Officers:*** Field Officers are officers holding the rank of Major (Mejar)

***Junior Officers:*** This group consists of Junior Lieutenant (Leftenan Muda), Lieutenant (Leftenan) and Captain (Kapten) grade officers.

### *Other Ranks*

This group begins at Private (Prebet) and works its way up to Warrant Officer I (Pegawai Waren I). This is further subdivided into 3 groups.

Senior NCO (PTT Kanan) This grouping includes NCOs holding the rank of Sergeant (Sarjan), Staff Sergeant (Staf Sarjan), Warrant Officer II (Pegawai Waren II) and Warrant Officer I (Pegawai Waren I).

Junior NCO (PTT Rendah) This grouping includes NCOs holding the rank of Lance Corporal (Lans Koperal) and Corporal (Koperal).

Private (Prebet) Private soldiers in the Malaysian Army do not wear any rank devices on their uniform. There are no distinctions made between junior or senior Privates.

### Corps and Regiments

- Rejimen Askar Melayu DiRaja (Royal Malay Regiment)
- Rejimen Renjer DiRaja (Royal Ranger Regiment)
- Rejimen Sempadan (Border Regiment)
- Kor Armor DiRaja (Royal Armoured Corps)
- Rejimen Artileri DiRaja (Royal Artillery Regiment)
- Rejimen Semboyan DiRaja (Royal Signals Regiment)
- Kor Perkhidmatan Am (General Services Corps)

- Kor Polis Tentera DiRaja (Royal Military Police Corps);
- Kor Kesihatan DiRaja (Royal Medical Corps)
- Kor Risik DiRaja (Royal Intelligence Corps)
- Kor Perkhidmatan DiRaja (Royal Logistics Corps);
- Kor Ordnans DiRaja (Royal Ordnance Corps)
- Rejimen Askar Jurutera DiRaja (Royal Engineer Regiment)
- Kor Jurutera Letrik dan Jentera DiRaja (Royal Electrical and Mechanical Engineer Corps)
- Kor Agama Angkatan Tentera (KAGAT)
- Rejimen Askar Wataniah (Territorial Army Regiment)
- Rejimen Gerak Khas (Special Forces Regiment)
- Pasukan Udara Tentera Darat (Army Air Corps)

***Combat Elements***

- *Rejimen Askar Melayu DiRaja (Royal Malay Regiment)*

  (i) Rejimen Askar Melayu DiRaja (Royal Malay Regiment) is the most senior regiment of the Malaysian Army. Its ranks are recruited from amongst the Malay population.

  (ii) The Regiment has 25 battalions which are configured as Standard Infantry Battalions (20 battalions), Mechanised Infantry Battalions (2 battalions), Parachute Infantry Battalions (2 battalions) or as Support Battalions (1 battalion). The 1st Battalion, the most senior in the Regiment, currently undertakes ceremonial and Royal Guard duties.

  (iiii) A unit of the Regiment, 19th Bn Royal Malay Regiment (Mech) was involved in the rescue of US Rangers and Delta Force operatives in

Somalia during the Battle of Mogadishu. The unit of 32 Radpanzer Condor APCs and 113 men from MALBATT 1 went in with the United States 10th Mountain Division to rescue the trapped rangers. Four APCs were immobilised and were destroyed by US helicopter gunships. 19 Royal Malay Regiment suffered 1 soldier killed in action (KIA), PFC Mat Aznan Awang while 8 others were wounded in action (WIA). Pfc Mat Aznan Awang was later promoted posthumously to Corporal and was awarded with Pingat Seri Pahlawan Gagah Perkasa, the nation's highest gallantry award. In total, 7 officers and 26 NCOs were awarded with various medals for their valour during the operation, the highest number of men recommended for medals in a single unit in a single operation.

(iv) RAMD Beret's color is dark green except two of army elite battalion wearing Maroon Beret.

- *Rejimen Renjer DiRaja (Royal Ranger Regiment)*

(a) Rejimen Renjer DiRaja (Royal Ranger Regiment) is a multi-racial unit organised along similar lines to the Rejimen Askar Melayu DiRaja. There are currently 9 Renjer battalions.

(b) The Regiment traces its roots to the Sarawak Rangers and the Sarawak Constabulary, famed jungle trackers who had a deadly reputation during the Malayan Emergency and during the Communist Party of Malaya's insurgency in Malaysia.

(c) The 8th Bn Royal Ranger Regiment (8 Renjer) was the first infantry battalion in the Malaysian Army to undergo conversion into an airborne battalion. The unit is currently assigned to the elite 10 Brigade (Para).

(d) The Malaysian Army's most decorated hero, WOI (Rtd) Kanang anak Langkau was a Regimental Sergeant Major of 8 Renjer.

- *Rejimen Sempadan (Border Regiment)*

(a) Rejimen Sempadan (Border Regiment) is a newly created regiment from the 300 series Territorial Army units in-charge of the border.

(b) As of 1 July 2006, the Deputy Prime Minister Defense Minister, Dato Seri Najib Tun Razak had announced the formation of a new regiment specifically for border patrol. Members of the regiment will be taken from the various regiments and corps, most notably from the Rejimen Askar Wataniah. The minister also added that the Rejimen Askar Wataniah 300 series. 500 series Regiments will be restructured in the near future to accommodate the formation of the Rejimen Pengurusan Sempadan. It is believed that the army will form about 2 to 3 brigades of this new regiment. The new regiment was officially materialised and launched on 9 February 2008 by Najib Tun Razak at the 1st Battalion RS, Tanah Merah, Kelantan.

- *Kor Armor DiRaja (Royal Armoured Corps)*

1. Kor Armor DiRaja (Royal Armour Corps) provides the armour capability for the Malaysian Army.
2. Currently, the Corps consists of 5 Battalions (sometimes errantly referred to as Regiments), which are equipped with various armoured personnel carriers (SIBMAS AFSV-90,Rheinmetall Condor, K-200 MIFV) and light combat vehicles.
3. The delivery of 48 PT-91M Main Battle Tanks from Poland has started in summer 2007 .

***Combat Support Element***

- *Rejimen Artileri DiRaja (Royal Artillery Regiment)*
  - (a) Rejimen Artileri DiRaja (Royal Artillery Regiment) is the artillery corps of the Malaysian Army and provides artillery support and local air defense for army units.
  - (b) The regiment is equipped with 36 Brazilian-made Astros II multiple launch rocket systems (MLRS) and the 28 G5 MkIII towed artillery guns from South Africa. Air defense is provided using a mix of Swiss Oerlikon twin 35 mm and Swedish Bofors 40 mm anti-aircraft artillery and missile systems such as the Jernas and Starburst from the UK; Anza from Pakistan;FN-6 from China and Igla from Russia.
- *Rejimen Semboyan DiRaja (Royal Signals Regiment)*
  - o Rejimen Semboyan DiRaja (Royal Signals Regiment) is in charge of strategic communications, tactical communications, electronic warfare and early warning systems such as radar.
- *Kor Polis Tentera DiRaja (Royal Military Police Corps)*
  - o Kor Polis Tentera DiRaja (Royal Military Police Corps) deploy as part of the field army in support of army operations and enforces proper conduct among army personnel. Aside from being responsible for base security, the military police are also tasked with preventing and investigating criminal activities on army property or by military personnel.
- *Rejimen Askar Jurutera DiRaja (Royal Engineers Regiment)*
  - o Rejimen Askar Jurutera DiRaja (Royal Engineers Regiment) is tasked with demolitions,

bridge-laying and the repair of military infrastructure such as airbase runways or clearing obstacles in emergency situations.

- *Kor Jurutera Elektrik dan Jentera DiRaja (Royal Electrical and Mechanical Engineers Corps)*
  - o Kor Jurutera Elektrik dan Jentera DiRaja (Royal Electrical and Mechanical Engineers Corps) are responsible for the maintenance of all vehicles and machinery of the Malaysian Army.
- *Kor Risik DiRaja (Royal Intelligence Corps)*
  - o Kor Risik DiRaja (Royal Intelligence Corps) specializes in psychological warfare (psyops), surveillance, espionage, reconnaissance and counter-intelligence operations. Aside from handling propaganda and counter-propaganda, the corps is also tasked with conducting background checks on recruits when they first enroll in any training courses.

***Support Elements***

- Kor Ordnans DiRaja (Royal Ordnance Corps)
  - o Kor Ordnans DiRaja (Royal Ordnance Corps) ensures that all military supplies and ordnance are stored, secured and inventoried properly.
- Kor Agama Angkatan Tentera (Armed Forces Religious Corp)
  - o Kor Agama Angkatan Tentera (Armed Forces Religious Corp) (KAGAT) performs religious (chaplainry) services for Muslim and Christian army personnel of the Malaysian Army. They also provide counselling and conduct ritual prayers on the battlefield.
- Kor Perkhidmatan DiRaja (Royal Logistics Corps)
  - o Kor Perkhidmatan DiRaja (Royal Logistics

Corps) is in charge of ferrying troops and supplies to the various units of the Malaysian Army.

- Kor Kesihatan DiRaja (Royal Medical Corps)
  - o Kor Kesihatan DiRaja (Royal Medical Corps) provides training for Army medics and other specialists. It runs the Armed Forces hospitals and provides the battlefield mobile hospitals. The unit has also provided relief MALMEDTIMs (Malaysian Medical Teams) to Pakistan, Afghanistan, West Sahara, Indonesia and Palestine.
- Kor Perkhidmatan Am (General Services Corps)
  - o Kor Perkhidmatan Am (General Services Corps) is a branch of Malaysian Army that handles administration and financial management of the entire army.

***Special Forces***

- Rejimen Gerak Khas
  - (a) Rejimen Gerak Khas (Special Forces Regiment) is the special forces and commando regiment of the Malaysian Army. 21 Gerup Gerak Khas is the operational home of various specialists and the Commando battalions which are capable of conducting unconventional warfare or special operations.
  - (b) One of the known foreign operations involving this regiment was an attack by Somali militia on a convoy transporting UN Intelligence Chief in UNOSOM II on 18 July 1994. In the action, 2 members of the regiment were killed in action while another 4 were wounded. One of the injured men was taken hostage by the militia and was released 9 hours later.

- Pasukan Udara Tentera Darat
  - Pasukan Udara Tentera Darat (Army Air Corps) is the Army Aviation branch formed around a core of Royal Malaysian Air Force officers.
  - This new Army formation is tasked with liaison duties, provides limited transportation capabilities, close air support and also air reconnaissance using light observation helicopters.

The unit currently has one squadron, No. 881 Squadron, equipped with 11 Agusta A109 LOH and 10 SA 316 Alouette III light helicopters. The main Army Air Corps base is located in Kluang, Johor.

***Reserves***

- Rejimen Askar Wataniah (Territorial Army)
  - Rejimen Askar Wataniah (Territorial Army) forms the second line of Malaysia's defence. Formed by college students, professionals and civilians, they provide support for the regular armed forces of Malaysia and are responsible for the security of key installations in times of conflict. Originally tasked with area and local defence, the Rejimen Askar Wataniah units have been reconfigured and will perform front line duties alongside regular units when the need arises. Rejimen Askar Wataniah units such as armored squadrons are integral units of several Kor Armor DiRaja regiments.

**Strength and Equipment**

Present strength of the Malaysian Army is approximately as follows:

Malaysian Army Active: 110,000 personnel

Active Reserve: 41,600 personnel

Paramilitary: 18,000 personnel

RELA People's volunteer corps:596,799 personnel

5 infantry divisions, formed from 12 infantry brigades, 1 parachute brigade and 1 mechanised brigade. The 3rd Division ("Sehitam, Semerah") is converting to become the army's first combined arms formation.

- 26 Light Infantry Battalions
- 3 Airborne Infantry Battalions
- 3 Mechanized Infantry Battalions
- 5 Armoured Regiments (1 Tank Regiment)
- 16 Artillery Regiments (4 Low Level Air Defence)
- 3 Special Forces Regiments

Approximately 60 Infantry (Askar Wataniah) Battalions.

Like most armed forces in the world, the Malaysian Army is in possession of numerous other weapons, mostly to be used by special forces units such as the *Grup Gerak Khas* or by soldiers with a special assignment such as snipers.

| *Missile Weapons Air-Defense Types* | *Origin* | *Versions* | *Quantity* | *Notes* |
|---|---|---|---|---|
| MBDA Rapier missile | United Kingdom | Jernas | 150 | - |
| Starburst surface-to-air missile | United Kingdom | Standard | 504 | VML / LML Launchers |
| Fei Nu-6 | People's Republic of China | Standard | Not Known | - |
| Anza (missile) | Pakistan | Mk. II | 160 | - |
| 9K38 Igla | Russia | SA-18 | 382 | Man-portable air-defence systems. |
| **Anti Tank Types** | | | | |
| **Baktar-Shikan** | **Pakistan** | **Standard** | **450** | |
| **MBDA ERYX** | **France** | **Standard** | **274** | |
| **Saab Bofors Dynamics AT4** | **Sweden** | **Standard** | **Not Known** | |
| **C-90 CR (M3)** | **Spain** | **RB LAW** | **Not Known** | - |
| **Carl Gustav recoilless rifle** | **Sweden** | **M2** | **Not Known** | - |
| **M40 recoilless rifle** | **United States** | **Standard** | **Not Known** | - |

| Artillery Types | | | | |
|---|---|---|---|---|
| Astros II MLRS | Brazil | Keris 300 mm | 36 | not including 10× AV-VBL Artillery Command Vehicles |
| Denel G5 howitzer | South Africa | Howitzer Mk.3 | 22 | |
| VSEL FH-70 | United Kingdom | Standard | 12 | - |
| OTO Melara Mod 56 | Italy | Standard | Not Known | - |
| Oerlikon 35 mm twin cannon | Switzerland | Standard | 16 | - |
| Bofors 40 mm gun | Sweden | Standard | Not Known | - |

## Recent Developments

After the recovery from the 1997 economic crisis, MA along with other branches of the MAF regains momentum in its modernizing programs. The first major procurement was to set a milestone by building its first ever main battle tank regiment. MA received delivery of 48 PT-91M main battle tanks and other tank based equipment like ARV WZT-4 from Poland, fully completed contract of sale in March 2010. Despite adding some 28 units of South African G5 Mk III 155 mm howitzers, another major procurement was 18 units of Astros MRLS from Brazil which delivery was completed in 2006. A second batch of 18 units MLRS was ordered in 2007. MA is also rapidly mechanizing its current inventory where 211 Adnan IFVs (Infantry Fighting Vehicle) has been acquired by the army in 2004. Following a more recent procurement of the Pakistani Bakhtar-Shikan Anti-armor missile launcher, these were installed on the Adnans.

MA is now shifting its emphasis on enhancing its air wing. In September, 2006, MA had received its 11th and last Agusta-Westland A109H Light Utility Helicopter. These helicopters are to initially complement and ultimately replace the aging SA316B Aérospatiale Alouette III helicopters. 6 of them were to be installed with light arms and to be tasked to a scout observation unit; a sample was shown in LIMA 07. The configuration of the remainder is unclear.

Furthermore, the army will also receive S61A-4 Nuri multipurpose helicopters after they are retired from RMAF to form the backbone for the army's very first air transport unit. These helicopters will form the army air wing's squadron 881 and squadron 882 respectively.

The same year at the biannual Defence Services Asia (DSA) 2006, Malaysia announced the U.S. made M4 Carbine service rifle will replace the Austrian made Steyr AUG service rifle for all three Malaysian Armed Forces services. The army will eventually receive the new weapon soon.

There is also a requirement for an upgrade to the current air defence network. However a dispute between the army and the air force on whether to introduce a mid-range SAM system had led the procurement to be on hold. According to a recent interview of the army's chief of staff, Ismail bin Haji Jamaluddin, the army has no intention to take over the mid range air defence role.

## REFERENCES

Astros II Artillery Saturation Rocket System Army Technology.

Jakarta Post article broken since 16 nov 2007.

"Malaysia pledges Lebanon troops". *news.bbc.co.uk*. 4 August 2006. http://news.bbc.co.uk/2/hi/asia-pacific/5244616.stm. Retrieved 12 August 2006.

Three Southeast Asian armies ready to deploy to Lebanon.

The Star article broken since 16-11-2007.

# Appendices

## APPENDIX-1

### SAARC REGIONAL CONVENTION ON SUPPRESSION OF TERRORISM, 1986

THE MEMBER STATES OF THE SOUTH ASIAN ASSOCIATION FOR REGIONAL COOPERATION (SAARC)

*Mindful* of the principles of cooperation enshrined in the SAARC Charter;

*Recalling* that at the Dhaka Summit on December 7-8, 1985, the Heads of State or Government of the Member States of the SAARC recognized the seriousness of the problem of terrorism as it alleets the security and stability of the region;

*Also recalling* the Bangalore Summit Declaration of 1 of 17 November 1986, in which the Heads of state or Government of SAARC agreed that cooperation among SAARC States was vital if terrorism was to be prevented and eliminated from the region; unequivocally condemned all acts, methods and practices of terrorism as criminal and deplored their impact on life and property, socio-economic development, political stability, regional and international peace and cooperation, and recognized the importance ot the principles laid down in UN Resolution 2625 (XXV) which among others required that each state should refrain from organizing, instigating, assisting or participating in acts of civil strife or terrorist acts in another state or acquiescing in organized activities within its territory directed towards the commission of such acts;

*Aware* of the danger posed by the spread of terrorism and its harmful effect on peace, cooperation, friendship and good neighbourly relations and which could also jeopardize the sovereignty and territorial integrity of states;

*Have Resolved* to take effective measures to ensure that perpetrators ol terroristic acts do not escape prosecution and punishment by providing for their extradition or prosecution, and to this end,

*Have agreed* as follows:

**Article I**

Subject to the overall requirements of the law of extradition, conduct constituting any of the following offences, according to the law of the Contracting State, shall be regarded as terroristic and for the purpose of extradition shall not be regarded as political offence or as an offence connected with a political olfence or as an offence inspired by political motives:

a. An offence within the scope of the Convention for the Suppression of Unlawful Sei/ure ol Aircraft, signed at the Hague on December 16, 1 970;
b. An offence within the scope of the Convention lor the Suppression of Unlawtul acts against the safety of Civil Aviation, signed at Montreal on September 23,1971;
c. An offence within the scope of the Convention on the Prevention and Punishment of Crimes against Internationally Protected Persons, including Diplomatic Agents, signed at New York on December 14, 1973;
d. An offence within the scope ol any Convention to which SAARC Member Sales concerned aie parties

and which obliges the parties to prosecute or grant extradition;

e. Murder, manslaughter, assault causing bodily harm, kidnapping, hostage-taking and oilences relating to firearms, weapons, explosives and dangerous substances when used as a means to perpetrate indiscriminate violence involving death or serious bodily injury to persons or serious damage to property;

An attempt or conspiracy to commit an offence described in sub-Paragraphs (a) to (el, aiding, abetting or counseling the commission of such an offence or participating as an accomplice in the offences so described.

**Article II**

For the purpose of extradition between SAARC Member States, any two or more Contracting Slates may, by agreement, decide to include any other serious offence involving violence, which shall not be regarded as a political offence or an offence connected with a political offence or an offence inspired by political motives.

**Article III**

1. The provisions of all extradition treaties and arrangements applicable between Contracting States are hereby amended as between Contracting States to the extent that they are incompatible with this Convention.

2. For the purpose of this Convention and to the extent that any offence referred to in Article I or agreed to in terms of Article II is not listed as an extraditable offence in any extradition treaty existing between Contracting States, it shall be deemed to be included as such therein.

3. Contracting States undertake to include these offences as extraditable offences in any future extradition treaty to be concluded between them.

4. If a Contracting State which makes extradition

conditional on the existence of a treaty receives a request for extradition from another Contracting State with which it has no extradition treaty, the requested State may, as its option, consider this Convention as the basis for extradition in respect ol the offences set lorth in Article I or agreed to in terms of Article II. Extradition shall be subject to the law of the requested State.

5. Contracting States, which do not make extradition conditional on the existence ol a treaty, shall recognize the offences set forth in Article I or agreed to in terms of Article II as extraditable oltences between themselves, subject to the law of the requested State.

**Article IV**

A contracting State in whose territory a person suspected of having committed an offence relerred to in Article I or agreed to in terms of Article II is found and which has received a request for extradition Irom another Contracting State, shall, if it does not extradite that person, submit the case without exception and without delay, to its competent authorities shall take their decisions in the same manner as in the case ol any offence of a serious nature under the law of the State.

**Article V**

For the purpose of Article IV, each Contracting State may take such measures as it deems appropriate, consistent with its national laws, subject to reciprocity, to exercise its jurisdiction in the case of an oiience under Article I or agreed to in terms of Article II.

**Article VI**

A Contracting State in whose territory an alleged offender is found, shall, upon receiving a request for extradition from another Contracting State, take appropriate measures, subject to its national laws, so as to ensure his presence for purposes of extradition or prosecution. Such measures shall immediately be notitied to the requesting State.

**Article VII**

Contracting States shall not be obliged to extradite, if it appears to the requested State that by reason of the trivial nature of the case or by reason of the request for the surrender or return of a fugitive offender not being made in good faith or in the interests of justice or for any other reason it is unjust or inexpedient to 2 of 3 surrender or return the fugitive offender.

**Article VIII**

1. Contracting States shall, subject to their national laws, afford one another the greatest measure ol mutual assistance in connection with proceedings brought in respect of the offences referred to in Article I or agree to in terms of Article II, including the supply of all evidence at their disposal necessary for the proceedings.

2. Contracting States shall cooperate among themselves, to the extent permitted by their national laws, through consultations between appropriate agencies, exchange of information, intelligence and expertise and such other cooperative measures as may be appropriate, with a view to prevention terroristic activities through precautionary measures.

**Article IX**

1. The Convention shall be open for signature by the Member States of SAARC at the SAARC Secretariat in Kathmandu.

2. It shall be subject to ratification. Instruments of ratification shall be deposited with the Secretary-General of SAARC.

**Article X**

The Convention shall enter into force on the fifteenth

day following the date of the deposit of the seventh Instrument of Ratification with Secretary-General of SAARC.

**Article XI**

The Secretary-General of SAARC shall be the depositary of this Convention and shall notily Member States of signatures to this Convention and all deposits of Instruments of Ratification. The Secretary-General shall transmit certified copies of such Instruments to each Member State. The Secretary-General shall also inform Member States of the date on which this Convention will have entered into force in accordance with Article X.

*In witness whereof* the undersigned, being duly authorized thereto by their respective Governments have signed this Convention.

*Done* at Kathmandu on this Fourth Day of November One Thousand Nine Hundred and Eighty Seven in eight originals in the English language all texts being equally authentic.

# APPENDIX–2

## Countriwise Military Expenditure (2009)

| Rank | Country | Military expenditure | % of GDP, 2008 |
|---|---|---|---|
| 1 | United States | 663,255,000,000 | 4.3% |
| 2 | China | 98,800,000,000 | 2.0% |
| 3 | United Kingdom | 69,271,000,000 | 2.5% |
| 4 | France | 67,316,000,000 | 2.3% |
| 5 | Russian Federation | 61,000,000,000 | 3.5% |
| 6 | Germany | 48,022,000,000 | 1.3% |
| 7 | Japan | 46,859,000,000 | 0.9% |
| 8 | Saudi Arabia | 39,257,000,000 | 8.2% |
| 9 | Italy | 37,427,000,000 | 1.7% |
| 10 | India | 36,600,000,000 | 2.6% |
| 11 | South Korea | 27,130,000,000 | 2.8% |
| 12 | Brazil | 27,124,000,000 | 1.5% |
| 13 | Canada | 20,564,000,000 | 1.3% |
| 14 | Australia | 20,109,000,000 | 1.8% |
| 15 | Spain | 19,409,000,000 | 1.2% |
| 16 | Turkey | 19,009,000,000 | 2.2% |
| 17 | Israel | 14,309,000,000 | 7.0% |
| 18 | Greece | 13,917,000,000 | 3.6% |
| 19 | United Arab Emirates | 13,052,000,000 | 5.9% |
| 20 | Netherlands | 12,642,000,000 | 1.4% |
| 21 | Poland | 10,860,000,000 | 2.0% |
| 22 | Colombia | 10,055,000,000 | 3.7% |
| 23 | Republic of China (Taiwan) | 9,866,000,000 | 2.1% |
| 24 | Iran | 9,174,000,000 | 2.7% |
| 25 | Singapore | 7,966,000,000 | 4.1% |
| 26 | Sweden | 6,135,000,000 | 1.3% |
| 27 | Norway | 6,098,000,000 | 1.3% |
| 28 | Chile | 5,683,000,000 | 3.5% |
| 29 | Algeria | 5,677,000,000 | 3.0% |
| 30 | Belgium | 5,674,000,000 | 1.2% |
| 31 | Mexico | 5,490,000,000 | 0.5% |
| 32 | Indonesia | 4,908,000,000 | 1.0% |

| | | | |
|---|---|---|---|
| 33 | Thailand | 4,908,000,000 | 1.5% |
| 34 | Portugal | 4,884,000,000 | 2.0% |
| 35 | Pakistan | 4,823,000,000 | 2.6% |
| 36 | Kuwait | 4,589,000,000 | 3.2% |
| 37 | Denmark | 4,476,000,000 | 1.4% |
| 38 | Ukraine | 4,258,000,000 | 2.7% |
| 39 | Switzerland | 4,141,000,000 | 0.8% |
| 40 | Malaysia | 4,078,000,000 | 2.0% |
| 41 | Oman | 4,003,000,000 | 7.7% |
| 42 | South Africa | 3,926,000,000 | 1.3% |
| 43 | Iraq | 3,814,000,000 | 5.4% |
| 44 | Finland | 3,768,000,000 | 1.3% |
| 45 | Egypt | 3,665,000,000 | 2.3% |
| 46 | Austria | 3,650,000,000 | 0.9% |
| 47 | Venezuela | 3,254,000,000 | 1.4% |
| 48 | Czech Republic | 3,246,000,000 | 1.3% |
| 49 | Morocco | 3,143,000,000 | 3.4% |
| 50 | Angola | 2,893,000,000 | 3.0% |
| 51 | Romania | 2,616,000,000 | 1.5% |
| 52 | Argentina | 2,608,000,000 | 0.8% |
| 53 | Vietnam | 2,073,000,000 | 2.4% |
| 54 | Sudan | 1,971,000,000[c] | 4.4% |
| 55 | Hungary | 1,900,000,000 | 1.2% |
| 56 | Syria | 1,883,000,000 | 3.4% |
| 57 | Nigeria | 1,681,000,000 | 0.8% |
| 58 | Ireland | 1,581,000,000 | 0.6% |
| 59 | Kazakhstan | 1,540,000,000 | 1.2% |
| 60 | Sri Lanka | 1,525,000,000 | 3.6% |
| 61 | Peru | 1,502,000,000 | 1.1% |
| 62 | New Zealand | 1,447,000,000 | 1.1% |
| 63 | Azerbaijan | 1,434,000,000 | 3.8% |
| 64 | Philippines | 1,424,000,000 | 0.8% |
| 65 | Lebanon | 1,408,000,000 | 3.9% |
| 66 | Jordan | 1,392,000,000 | 5.9% |
| 67 | Slovakia | 1,316,000,000 | 1.5% |
| 68 | Yemen | 1,196,000,000 | 4.2% |

| | | | |
|---|---|---|---|
| 69 | Croatia | 1,191,000,000 | 1.9% |
| 70 | Bulgaria | 1,127,000,000 | 2.4% |
| 71 | Libya | 1,100,000,000 | 1.0% |
| 72 | Serbia | 1,070,000,000 | 2.4% |
| 73 | Belarus | 1,036,000,000 | 1.5% |
| 74 | Bangladesh | 938,000,000 | 1.0% |
| 75 | Slovenia | 888,000,000 | 1.5% |
| 76 | Bahrain | 721,000,000 | 3.0% |
| 77 | Latvia | 692,000,000 | 1.9% |
| 78 | Georgia | 665,000,000 | 8.5% |
| 79 | Lithuania | 648,000,000 | 1.5% |
| 80 | Tunisia | 571,000,000 | 1.3% |
| 81 | Cyprus | 550,000,000 | 1.8% |
| 82 | Kenya | 518,000,000 | 1.9% |
| 83 | Uruguay | 496,000,000 | 1.3% |
| 84 | Estonia | 460,000,000 | 2.2% |
| 85 | Ethiopia | 422,000,000 | 1.4% |
| 86 | Chad | 412,000,000 | 6.6% |
| 87 | Luxembourg | 406,000,000 | 0.7% |
| 88 | Armenia | 405,000,000 | 3.3% |
| 89 | Côte d'Ivoire | 369,000,000 | 1.5% |
| 90 | Botswana | 353,000,000 | 2.7% |
| 91 | Cameroon | 352,000,000 | 1.5% |
| 92 | Uganda | 341,000,000 | 2.3% |
| 93 | Brunei | 336,000,000 | 3.9% |
| 94 | Eritrea | 327,000,000 | 20.9% |
| 95 | Namibia | 283,000,000 | 3.5% |
| 96 | Albania | 276,000,000 | 2.0% |
| 97 | Bosnia and Herzegovina | 276,000,000 | 1.4% |
| 98 | Afghanistan | 272,000,000 | 1.9% |
| 99 | Dominican Republic | 272,000,000 | 0.6% |
| 100 | Bolivia | 268,000,000 | 1.5% |
| 101 | Zambia | 251,000,000 | 2.0% |
| 102 | Turkmenistan | 236,000,000 | 2.9% |
| 103 | Senegal | 217,000,000 | 1.6% |
| 104 | Tanzania | 216,000,000 | 1.1% |

| | | | |
|---|---|---|---|
| 105 | Republic of Macedonia | 204,000,000 | 1.8% |
| 106 | Nepal | 194,000,000 | 2.0% |
| 107 | Kyrgyzstan | 185,000,000 | 3.7% |
| 108 | Mali | 182,000,000 | 1.9% |
| 109 | Guatemala | 175,000,000 | 0.4% |
| 110 | Congo, Republic of the | 142,000,000[a] | 1.1% |
| 111 | Paraguay | 140,000,000 | 0.8% |
| 112 | Panama | 138,000,000 | 1.0% |
| 113 | El Salvador | 134,000,000 | 0.5% |
| 114 | Congo, Democratic Republic of the | 127,000,000 | 1.4% |
| 115 | Ghana | 127,000,000 | 0.7% |
| 116 | Cambodia | 123,000,000 | 1.1% |
| 117 | Mauritania | 122,000,000 | 3.7% |
| 118 | Burkina Faso | 112,000,000 | 1.4% |
| 119 | Honduras | 105,000,000 | 0.8% |
| 120 | Madagascar | 103,000,000 | 1.1% |
| 121 | Guinea | 99,800,000 | 2.2% |
| 122 | Mozambique | 92,500,000 | 0.8% |
| 123 | Jamaica | 80,300,000 | 0.6% |
| 124 | Rwanda | 72,700,000 | 1.5% |
| 125 | Mongolia | 71,000,000 | 1.4% |
| 126 | Benin | 67,700,000 | 1.1% |
| 127 | Tajikistan | 63,400,000 | 2.2% |
| 128 | Swaziland | 60,000,000 | 1.9% |
| 129 | Togo | 57,000,000 | 1.9% |
| 130 | Uzbekistan | 52,000,000 | 1.9% |
| 131 | Malta | 51,600,000 | 0.7% |
| 132 | Fiji | 48,400,000 | 1.3% |
| 133 | Malawi | 45,100,000 | 1.5% |
| 134 | Sierra Leone | 44,600,000 | 2.4% |
| 135 | Burundi | 43,900,000 | 4.0% |
| 136 | Lesotho | 43,600,000 | 1.6% |
| 137 | Niger | 43,000,000 | 0.5% |
| 138 | Nicaragua | 41,700,000 | 0.7% |
| 139 | Papua New Guinea | 37,200,000 | 0.4% |

| | | | |
|---|---|---|---|
| 140 | Central African Republic | 36,700,000 | 1.6% |
| 141 | Djibouti | 36,300,000 | 3.7% |
| 142 | Moldova | 27,500,000 | 0.6% |
| 143 | Laos | 21,200,000 | 0.4% |
| 144 | Guinea-Bissau | 16,800,000 | 3.8% |
| 145 | Belize | 15,600,000 | 1.1% |
| 146 | Mauritius | 15,300,000 | 0.2% |
| 147 | Cape Verde | 8,800,000 | 0.5% |
| 148 | Guyana | 7,900,000 | 0.8% |
| 149 | Liberia | 7,100,000 | 0.6% |
| 150 | Seychelles | 6,600,000 | 1.3% |
| 151 | Gambia, The | 5,300,000 | 0.5% |
| 152 | Zimbabwe | Not reported | 1.9% |

| *Rank* | *Country* | *2009 Spending ($ b.)* | *Share of 2008 GDP (%)* | *World Share (%)* |
|---|---|---|---|---|
| — | **World Total** | **1531** | **2.7** | **100** |
| 1 | United States | 661 | 4.3 | 43 |
| 2 | China | 100 | 2.0* | 6.6* |
| 3 | France | 63.9 | 2.3 | 4.2 |
| 4 | United Kingdom | 58.3 | 2.5 | 3.8 |
| 5 | Russia | 53.3 | 3.5* | 3.5* |
| 6 | Japan | 51.0 | 0.9 | 3.3 |
| 7 | Germany | 45.6 | 1.3 | 3.0 |
| 8 | Saudi Arabia** | 41.3 | 8.2 | 2.7 |
| 9 | India | 36.3 | 2.6 | 2.4 |
| 10 | Italy | 35.8 | 1.7 | 2.3 |
| 11 | Brazil | 26.1 | 1.5 | 1.7 |
| 12 | South Korea | 24.1 | 2.8 | 1.6 |
| 13 | Canada | 19.2 | 1.3 | 1.3 |
| 14 | Australia | 19.0 | 1.8 | 1.2 |
| 15 | Spain | 18.3 | 1.2 | 1.2 |

* SIPRI estimate

** The figures for Saudi Arabia include expenditure for public order and safety and might be slight overestimates.

*Source:* SIPRI Yearbook, 2010.

## Country-wise Strength of Armed Forces

| *State* | *Active* | *Reserve* | *Para-military* | *Total* | *Total per 1000 capita* | *Active per 1000 capita* |
|---|---|---|---|---|---|---|
| 1 | 2 | 3 | 4 | 5 | 6 | 7 |
| Afghanistan | 93,800 | 0 | 0 | 93,800 | 3.3 | 3.3 |
| Albania | 14,295 | 0 | 500 | 14,795 | 4.1 | 3.9 |
| Algeria | 147,000 | 150,000 | 187,200 | 484,200 | 14.2 | 4.3 |
| Angola | 107,000 | 0 | 10,000 | 117,000 | 9.1 | 8.4 |
| Antigua and Barbuda | 170 | 75 | 0 | 245 | 2.9 | 2 |
| Argentina | 73,100 | 0 | 31,240 | 104,340 | 2.6 | 1.8 |
| Armenia | 46,684 | 210,000 | 4,748 | 261,432 | 88.1 | 15.7 |
| Australia | 54,747 | 19,915 | 0 | 74,662 | 3.5 | 2.6 |
| Austria | 27,300 | 195,000 | 9,400 | 231,700 | 28.2 | 3.3 |
| Azerbaijan | 66,940 | 300,000 | 15,000 | 381,940 | 46.4 | 8.1 |
| Bahamas | 860 | 0 | 0 | 860 | 2.8 | 2.8 |
| Bahrain | 8,200 | 0 | 11,260 | 19,460 | 26.7 | 11.3 |
| Bangladesh | 157,053 | 0 | 63,900 | 220,953 | 1.4 | 1 |
| Barbados | 610 | 430 | 0 | 1,040 | 3.7 | 2.1 |
| Belarus | 72,940 | 289,500 | 110,000 | 472,440 | 49 | 7.6 |
| Belgium | 38,452 | 2,040 | 0 | 40,492 | 3.9 | 3.7 |
| Belize | 1,050 | 700 | 0 | 1,750 | 5.7 | 3.4 |
| Benin | 4,750 | 0 | 2,500 | 7,250 | 0.8 | 0.5 |
| Bolivia | 46,100 | 0 | 37,100 | 83,200 | 8.5 | 4.7 |
| Bosnia and Herzegovina | 11,099 | 0 | 0 | 11,099 | 2.4 | 2.4 |
| Botswana | 9,000 | 0 | 1,500 | 10,500 | 5.3 | 4.5 |
| Brazil | 327,710 | 1,340,000 | 395,000 | 2,062,710 | 10.4 | 1.6 |
| Brunei | 7,000 | 700 | 2,250 | 9,950 | 25.6 | 18 |
| Bulgaria | 34,975 | 302,500 | 34,000 | 371,475 | 51.6 | 4.9 |
| Burkina Faso | 11,200 | 0 | 250 | 11,450 | 0.7 | 0.7 |
| Burundi | 20,000 | 0 | 31,050 | 51,050 | 5.4 | 2.1 |
| Cambodia | 124,300 | 0 | 67,000 | 191,300 | 13.2 | 8.6 |
| Cameroon | 14,100 | 0 | 9,000 | 23,100 | 1.2 | 0.7 |
| Canada | 65,722 | 33,967 | 4,554 | 104,243 | 3.1 | 2 |
| Cape Verde | 1,200 | 0 | 0 | 1,200 | 2.8 | 2.8 |
| Central African Republic | 2,150 | 0 | 1,000 | 3,150 | 0.7 | 0.5 |
| Chad | 25,350 | 0 | 9,500 | 34,850 | 3.4 | 2.5 |
| Chile | 60,560 | 40,000 | 41,500 | 142,060 | 8.6 | 3.6 |
| China | 2,285,000 | 510,000 | 660,000 | 3,455,000 | 2.6 | 1.7 |
| Colombia | 285,220 | 61,900 | 144,097 | 491,217 | 11.2 | 6.5 |
| Costa Rica | 0 | 0 | 9,800 | 9,800 | 2.3 | 0 |
| Croatia | 18,600 | 21,000 | 3,000 | 42,600 | 9.5 | 4.1 |

*contd....*

| 1 | 2 | 3 | 4 | 5 | 6 | 7 |
|---|---|---|---|---|---|---|
| Cuba | 49,000 | 1,159,000 | 26,500 | 1,234,500 | 107.8 | 4.3 |
| Cyprus | 10,050 | 50,000 | 750 | 60,800 | 56 | 9.3 |
| Czech Republic | 17,932 | 0 | 10,988 | 28,920 | 2.8 | 1.8 |
| Côte d'Ivoire | 17,050 | 10,000 | 1,500 | 28,550 | 1.4 | 0.8 |
| Democratic Republic of the Congo | 151,251 | 0 | 1,400 | 152,651 | 2.2 | 2.2 |
| Denmark | 26,585 | 53,507 | 0 | 80,092 | 14.6 | 4.8 |
| Djibouti | 10,450 | 0 | 2,500 | 12,950 | 17.9 | 14.4 |
| Dominican Republic | 49,910 | 0 | 15,000 | 64,910 | 6.7 | 5.2 |
| Ecuador | 57,983 | 118,000 | 400 | 176,383 | 12.1 | 4 |
| Egypt | 468,500 | 479,000 | 397,000 | 1,344,500 | 17 | 5.9 |
| El Salvador | 15,500 | 9,900 | 17,000 | 42,400 | 5.9 | 2.2 |
| Equatorial Guinea | 1,320 | 0 | 2,000 | 3,320 | 5.2 | 2.1 |
| Eritrea | 201,750 | 120,000 | 0 | 321,750 | 57 | 35.7 |
| Estonia | 4,750 | 25,000 | 10,766 | 40,516 | 31.2 | 3.7 |
| Ethiopia | 138,000 | 0 | 0 | 138,000 | 1.6 | 1.6 |
| Fiji | 3,500 | 6,000 | 0 | 9,500 | 10.1 | 3.7 |
| Finland | 22,600 | 361,500 | 7,550 | 391,650 | 74.6 | 4.3 |
| France | 352,771 | 70,300 | 46,390 | 469,461 | 7.3 | 5.5 |
| Gabon | 4,700 | 0 | 2,000 | 6,700 | 4.4 | 3.1 |
| Gambia | 800 | 0 | 0 | 800 | 0.4 | 0.4 |
| Georgia | 21,150 | 0 | 11,700 | 32,850 | 7.5 | 4.8 |
| Germany | 250,613 | 161,812 | 0 | 412,425 | 5 | 3 |
| Ghana | 15,500 | 0 | 0 | 15,500 | 0.6 | 0.6 |
| Greece | 156,600 | 237,500 | 4,000 | 398,100 | 37.1 | 14.6 |
| Guatemala | 15,212 | 63,863 | 18,536 | 97,611 | 7.4 | 1.1 |
| Guinea | 12,300 | 0 | 7,000 | 19,300 | 1.9 | 1.2 |
| Guinea-Bissau | 4,450 | 0 | 2,000 | 6,450 | 4.2 | 2.9 |
| Guyana | 1,100 | 670 | 1,500 | 3,270 | 4.3 | 1.5 |
| Haiti | 0 | 0 | 2,000 | 2,000 | 0.2 | 0 |
| Honduras | 12,000 | 60,000 | 8,000 | 80,000 | 10.2 | 1.5 |
| Hungary | 29,450 | 44,000 | 12,000 | 85,450 | 8.6 | 3 |
| Iceland | 0 | 0 | 130 | 130 | 0.4 | 0 |
| India | 1,325,000 | 2,142,821 | 1,300,586 | 4,768,407 | 4.1 | 1.1 |
| Indonesia | 302,000 | 400,000 | 280,000 | 982,000 | 4.1 | 1.3 |
| Iran | 523,000 | 1,800,000 | 60,000 | 2,383,000 | 35.9 | 7.9 |
| Iraq | 191,957 | 0 | 386,312 | 578,269 | 20 | 6.6 |
| Ireland | 10,460 | 14,875 | 0 | 25,335 | 6 | 2.5 |
| Israel | 176,500 | 565,000 | 8,050 | 749,550 | 103.6 | 24.4 |
| Italy | 293,202 | 41,867 | 142,933 | 478,002 | 8.2 | 5 |

*contd....*

| 1 | 2 | 3 | 4 | 5 | 6 | 7 |
|---|---|---|---|---|---|---|
| Jamaica | 2,830 | 953 | 0 | 3,783 | 1.3 | 1 |
| Japan | 230,300 | 41,800 | 12,250 | 284,350 | 2.2 | 1.8 |
| Jordan | 100,500 | 65,000 | 10,000 | 175,500 | 28 | 16 |
| Kazakhstan | 49,000 | 0 | 31,500 | 80,500 | 5.2 | 3.2 |
| Kenya | 24,120 | 0 | 5,000 | 29,120 | 0.7 | 0.6 |
| Kuwait | 15,500 | 23,700 | 7,100 | 46,300 | 17.2 | 5.8 |
| Kyrgyzstan | 10,900 | 0 | 9,500 | 20,400 | 3.8 | 2 |
| Laos | 29,100 | 0 | 100,000 | 129,100 | 18.9 | 4.3 |
| Latvia | 5,745 | 10,866 | 0 | 16,611 | 7.4 | 2.6 |
| Lebanon | 59,100 | 232,635 | 20,000 | 311,735 | 77.6 | 14.7 |
| Lesotho | 2,000 | 0 | 0 | 2,000 | 0.9 | 0.9 |
| Liberia | 2,400 | 0 | 0 | 2,400 | 0.7 | 0.7 |
| Libya | 76,000 | 40,000 | 0 | 116,000 | 18.3 | 12 |
| Lithuania | 8,850 | 6,700 | 14,600 | 30,150 | 8.5 | 2.5 |
| Luxembourg | 900 | 0 | 612 | 1,512 | 3.1 | 1.8 |
| Madagascar | 13,500 | 0 | 8,100 | 21,600 | 1 | 0.7 |
| Malawi | 5,300 | 0 | 1,500 | 6,800 | 0.5 | 0.4 |
| Malaysia | 109,000 | 296,300 | 24,600 | 429,900 | 16.7 | 4.2 |
| Mali | 7,350 | 0 | 7,800 | 15,150 | 1.1 | 0.5 |
| Malta | 1,954 | 167 | 0 | 2,121 | 5.2 | 4.8 |
| Mauritania | 15,870 | 0 | 5,000 | 20,870 | 6.7 | 5.1 |
| Mauritius | 0 | 0 | 2,000 | 2,000 | 1.6 | 0 |
| Mexico | 267,506 | 39,899 | 36,500 | 343,905 | 3.1 | 2.4 |
| Moldova | 5,998 | 66,000 | 2,379 | 74,377 | 17.2 | 1.4 |
| Mongolia | 10,000 | 137,000 | 7,200 | 154,200 | 50.7 | 3.3 |
| Montenegro | 3,127 | 0 | 10,100 | 13,227 | 19.7 | 4.7 |
| Morocco | 195,800 | 150,000 | 50,000 | 395,800 | 12.7 | 6.3 |
| Mozambique | 11,200 | 0 | 0 | 11,200 | 0.5 | 0.5 |
| Myanmar | 406,000 | 0 | 107,250 | 513,250 | 10.7 | 8.4 |
| Namibia | 9,200 | 0 | 6,000 | 15,200 | 7.2 | 4.4 |
| Nepal | 95,753 | 0 | 62,000 | 157,753 | 5.5 | 3.4 |
| Netherlands | 46,882 | 3,339 | 0 | 50,221 | 3 | 2.8 |
| New Zealand | 9,702 | 2,249 | 0 | 11,951 | 2.8 | 2.3 |
| Nicaragua | 12,000 | 0 | 0 | 12,000 | 2 | 2 |
| Niger | 5,300 | 0 | 5,400 | 10,700 | 0.7 | 0.3 |
| Nigeria | 80,000 | 0 | 82,000 | 162,000 | 1.1 | 0.5 |
| North Korea | 1,106,000 | 8,200,000 | 189,000 | 9,495,000 | 418.9 | 48.8 |
| Northern Cyprus | 5,000 | 26,000 | 150 | 31,150 | 117.5 | 18.9 |
| Norway | 24,025 | 45,250 | 0 | 69,275 | 14.9 | 5.2 |
| Oman | 42,600 | 0 | 4,400 | 47,000 | 13.8 | 12.5 |

*contd....*

| 1 | 2 | 3 | 4 | 5 | 6 | 7 |
|---|---|---|---|---|---|---|
| Pakistan | 617,000 | 0 | 304,000 | 921,000 | 5.3 | 3.5 |
| Palestine | 0 | 0 | 56,000 | 56,000 | 14 | 0 |
| Panama | 0 | 0 | 12,000 | 12,000 | 3.6 | 0 |
| Papua New Guinea | 3,100 | 0 | 0 | 3,100 | 0.5 | 0.5 |
| Paraguay | 10,650 | 164,500 | 14,800 | 189,950 | 27.2 | 1.5 |
| Peru | 114,000 | 195,000 | 77,000 | 386,000 | 13.1 | 3.9 |
| Philippines | 120,000 | 171,000 | 40,500 | 331,500 | 3.4 | 1.2 |
| Poland | 71,900 | 0 | 28,100 | 100,000 | 2.6 | 1.9 |
| Portugal | 43,330 | 210,900 | 47,700 | 301,930 | 28.2 | 4 |
| Qatar | 11,800 | 0 | 0 | 11,800 | 13.4 | 13.4 |
| Republic of Macedonia | 8,000 | 4,850 | 0 | 12,850 | 6.2 | 3.9 |
| Republic of the Congo | 10,000 | 0 | 2,000 | 12,000 | 3 | 2.5 |
| Romania | 73,350 | 45,000 | 79,900 | 198,250 | 8.9 | 3.3 |
| Russia | 1,027,000 | 20,000,000 | 449,000 | 21,476,000 | 153.4 | 7.3 |
| Rwanda | 33,000 | 0 | 2,000 | 35,000 | 3.3 | 3.1 |
| Saudi Arabia | 233,500 | 0 | 15,500 | 249,000 | 8.7 | 8.1 |
| Senegal | 13,620 | 0 | 5,000 | 18,620 | 1.4 | 1 |
| Serbia | 29,125 | 50,171 | 0 | 79,296 | 10.7 | 3.9 |
| Seychelles | 200 | 0 | 450 | 650 | 7.4 | 2.3 |
| Sierra Leone | 10,500 | 0 | 0 | 10,500 | 2 | 2 |
| Singapore | 72,500 | 356,500 | 93,800 | 522,800 | 112.2 | 15.6 |
| Slovakia | 16,531 | 0 | 0 | 16,531 | 3 | 3 |
| Slovenia | 7,200 | 3,800 | 4,500 | 15,500 | 7.7 | 3.6 |
| Somalia | 2,000 | 0 | 0 | 2,000 | 0.2 | 0.2 |
| Somaliland | 15,350 | 0 | 0 | 15,350 | 4.4 | 4.4 |
| South Africa | 62,082 | 15,071 | 12,382 | 89,535 | 1.8 | 1.3 |
| South Korea | 687,000 | 8,000,000 | 4,500 | 8,691,500 | 173.6 | 13.7 |
| Spain | 128,013 | 319,000 | 80,210 | 527,223 | 13 | 3.2 |
| Sri Lanka | 160,900 | 35,900 | 62,200 | 259,000 | 12.1 | 7.5 |
| Sudan | 109,300 | 85,000 | 17,500 | 211,800 | 5.2 | 2.7 |
| Suriname | 1,840 | 0 | 0 | 1,840 | 3.8 | 3.8 |
| Sweden | 13,050 | 242,000 | 800 | 255,850 | 28.2 | 1.4 |
| Switzerland | 22,059 | 174,071 | 80,000 | 276,130 | 36.3 | 2.9 |
| Syria | 325,000 | 314,000 | 108,000 | 747,000 | 34.3 | 14.9 |
| Taiwan | 290,000 | 1,657,000 | 17,000 | 1,964,000 | 85.5 | 12.6 |
| Tajikistan | 8,800 | 0 | 7,500 | 16,300 | 2.2 | 1.2 |
| Tanzania | 27,000 | 80,000 | 1,400 | 108,400 | 2.6 | 0.7 |
| Thailand | 305,860 | 245,000 | 113,700 | 664,560 | 10.1 | 4.6 |
| Timor Leste | 1,332 | 0 | 0 | 1,332 | 1.3 | 1.3 |
| Togo | 8,550 | 0 | 750 | 9,300 | 1.5 | 1.4 |
| Trinidad and Tobago | 4,063 | 0 | 0 | 4,063 | 3.3 | 3.3 |
| Tunisia | 35,800 | 0 | 12,000 | 47,800 | 4.6 | 3.4 |

*contd....*

| 1 | 2 | 3 | 4 | 5 | 6 | 7 |
|---|---|---|---|---|---|---|
| Turkey | 510,600 | 428,700 | 102,200 | 1,041,500 | 13.6 | 6.6 |
| Turkmenistan | 22,000 | 0 | 0 | 22,000 | 4.5 | 4.5 |
| Uganda | 45,000 | 0 | 1,800 | 46,800 | 1.4 | 1.4 |
| Ukraine | 129,925 | 1,000,000 | 84,900 | 1,214,825 | 26.6 | 2.8 |
| United Arab Emirates | 51,000 | 0 | 0 | 51,000 | 10.6 | 10.6 |
| United Kingdom | 175,690 | 199,280 | 0 | 374,970 | 6.1 | 2.9 |
| United States | 1,580,255 | 864,547 | 11,035 | 2,455,837 | 7.9 | 5.1 |
| Uruguay | 24,621 | 0 | 920 | 25,541 | 7.3 | 7 |
| Uzbekistan | 67,000 | 0 | 20,000 | 87,000 | 3.2 | 2.4 |
| Venezuela | 115,000 | 8,000 | 0 | 123,000 | 4.6 | 4.3 |
| Vietnam | 455,000 | 5,000,000 | 40,000 | 5,495,000 | 62 | 5.1 |
| Yemen | 66,700 | 0 | 71,200 | 137,900 | 6 | 2.9 |
| Zambia | 15,100 | 3,000 | 1,400 | 19,500 | 1.6 | 1.3 |
| Zimbabwe | 29,000 | 0 | 21,800 | 50,800 | 4.5 | 2.5 |

## Notes

1. The military members on active duty, that are currently serving full time in their military capacity.
2. The troops of the reserve force, that are not normally kept under arms and their main role is be available to fight when a nation mobilizes for emergency.
3. The paramilitary forces, armed units that are not considered part of a nation's formal military forces.

These numbers are approximations as military forces around the world are constantly changing in size.

Many of the 172 countries listed here, especially those with the highest number of total troops, such as the two Koreas and Vietnam, have included a large amount of paramilitaries, civilians and policemen into their reserve personnel. This is not the case of Russia, which still maintains reserve obligation from USSR times, that in its 20 million reservists includes only trained troops who have served during their life in the armed forces and must remain available until the age of 50 years. Some countries, such as Italy and Japan, have only volunteers into their armed forces; while others, such as Iceland and Panama, have no national armies, but only a paramilitary force.

## *APPENDIX 3*

# THE AUSTRALIA, NEW ZEALAND, UNITED STATES SECURITY TREATY (ANZUS)

The Australia, New Zealand, United States Security Treaty (ANZUS or ANZUS Treaty) is the military alliance which binds Australia and New Zealand and, separately, Australia and the United States to cooperate on defence matters in the Pacific Ocean area, though today the treaty is understood to relate to attacks in any area.

The treaty was previously a full three-way defence pact, but following a dispute between New Zealand and the United States in 1984 over visiting rights for nuclear-armed or nuclear-powered ships of the US Navy in New Zealand ports, the treaty no longer applies between the United States and New Zealand, but is still in force between either country and Australia, separately.

The Australia–US alliance under the ANZUS Treaty remains in full force. Heads of defence of one or both nations often have joined the annual ministerial meetings, which are supplemented by consultations between the US Combatant Commander Pacific and the Australian Chief of Defence Force. There are also regular civilian and military consultations between the two governments at lower levels. Annual meetings to discuss ANZUS defence matters take place between the United States Secretary of State and the Australian Minister for Foreign Affairs (AUSMIN). The most recent AUSMIN meeting took place in Washington in April 2009.

Unlike NATO, ANZUS has no integrated defence structure or dedicated forces. Nevertheless, Australia and the United States conduct a variety of joint activities. These include military exercises ranging from naval and landing exercises at the task-group level to battalion-level special forces training, assigning officers to each other's armed services, and standardising equipment and operational doctrine. The two countries also operate several joint defence facilities in Australia, mainly ground stations for early warning satellites, and signals intelligence gathering in South-East Asia and East Asia as part of the ECHELON network.

**Origins**

The treaty came about following the close cooperation of the United States, Australia and New Zealand during World War II, when Australia had come under attack by a foreign power, Japan, for the first time in its history. Following the end of World War II, the United States was eager to normalise relations with Japan, particularly as the Korean War was still raging a short distance from Japan. With the involvement of China and possibly the Soviet Union in Korea, the Cold War was threatening to become a full-scale war. However, Australia and New Zealand in particular were extremely reluctant to finalise a peace treaty with Japan which would allow for Japanese rearmament. Both countries relented only when an Australian and New Zealand proposal for a three-way security treaty was accepted by the United States.

The resulting treaty was concluded at San Francisco on 1 September 1951, and entered into force on 29 April 1952. The treaty bound the signatories to recognise that an armed attack in the Pacific area on any of them would endanger the peace and safety of the others. It stated 'The Parties will consult together whenever in the opinion of any of them the territorial integrity, political independence or security of any of the Parties is threatened in the Pacific'. The three nations also pledged to maintain and develop individual and collective capabilities to resist attack.

**Malaysia, Korea, Vietnam and The War on Terror**

The treaty itself was not a source of debate for 30 years, though in this period New Zealand and Australia committed forces to the Malayan Emergency and subsequently the ANZUS nations fought together in the Vietnam War.

As part of the United Nations deployment, New Zealand and Australia had earlier fought alongside the United States in the Korean War. Later New Zealand sent transport aircraft, maritime patrol aircraft and frigates to the Persian Gulf, as well as a very small number of soldiers, SAS soldiers, medical and assorted and peace-keeping forces in Afghanistan—and despite Prime Minister Helen Clark being openly critical of American justifications for the war, New Zealand did send engineer troops to Iraq during the 2003 invasion.

Australian reservations about the MX missile

In 1983, the United States approached Australia with proposals for testing the new generation of American intercontinental ballistic missiles, the MX missile. American test ranges in the Pacific were insufficient for testing the new long-range missiles and the United States military wished to use the Tasman Sea as a target area. Australian Prime Minister Malcolm Fraser of the Liberal Party had agreed to provide monitoring sites near Sydney for this purpose. However, in 1985 the United States released the new Prime Minister Bob Hawke of the Labor Party from this obligation after the agreement attracted significant criticism from the Left faction of the Labor Party.

**New Zealand Bans Nuclear Material**

In 1985, the nature of the ANZUS alliance changed significantly. Due to a current of anti-nuclear sentiment within New Zealand, tension had long been present between ANZUS members as the United States is a declared nuclear power. France, a naval power and a declared nuclear power, had been conducting nuclear tests on South Pacific Islands. Following the victory of the New Zealand Labour Party in elections in 1984, Prime Minister David Lange barred nuclear-powered or nuclear-armed ships from using New Zealand ports or entering New Zealand waters. Reasons given were the dangers of nuclear weapons, continued French nuclear testing in the South Pacific, and opposition to US President Ronald Reagan's policy of aggressively confronting the Soviet Union. Given that the United States Navy refused to confirm or deny the presence of nuclear weapons aboard ships, these laws essentially refused access to New Zealand ports for all United States Navy ships. In February 1985, a port-visit request by the United States for the USS *Buchanan* was refused by New Zealand, as the *Buchanan* was capable of launching nuclear depth bombs. According to opinion polls taken before the 1984 election, only 30 per cent of New Zealanders supported visits by US warships with a clear majority of 58 per cent opposed, and over 66 per cent of the population lived in locally declared nuclear free zones. An opinion poll commissioned by the 1986 Defence Committee of Enquiry confirmed that 92 per cent now opposed nuclear weapons in New Zealand and 69 per cent opposed warship visits; 92 per cent wanted New Zealand to promote nuclear disarmament through the UN, while 88 per cent supported the promotion of nuclear free zones.

**United States Suspends Obligations to New Zealand**

After consultations with Australia and after negotiations with New Zealand broke down, the United States announced that it was suspending its treaty obligations to New Zealand until United States Navy ships were re-admitted to New Zealand ports, citing that New Zealand was "a friend, but not an ally". The crisis made front-page headlines for weeks in many American newspapers, while many American cabinet members were quoted as expressing a deep sense of betrayal. However, David Lange did not withdraw New Zealand from ANZUS, although his government's policy led to the US's decision to suspend its treaty obligations to New Zealand.

An opinion poll in New Zealand in 1991 showed 54% of those sampled preferred to let the treaty lapse rather than accept visits again by nuclear-armed or nuclear-powered vessels. The policy did not become law until June 8, 1987 with the passing of the New Zealand Nuclear Free Zone, Disarmament, and Arms Control Act 1987, more than two years after the *Buchanan* was refused entry after the USA refused to declare the presence or absence of nuclear weapons, and a year after the USA suspended its treaty obligations to New Zealand.

On July 10, 1985, the French DGSE bombed the Greenpeace protest vessel *Rainbow Warrior* in Auckland. This event strengthened opposition in New Zealand of the military application of nuclear technology in any form. The failure of Western leaders to condemn what could be considered an act of war on New Zealand by France caused a great deal of change in foreign and defence policy. New Zealand distanced itself from its traditional ally, the United States, and built relationships with small South Pacific nations, while retaining its good relations with Australia, and, to a lesser extent, the United Kingdom.

For 11 September 2001 Attacks Australia and New Zealand both provided military units, including special forces and naval ships in support of the US led "Operation Enduring Freedom" (support for anti-Taliban forces in the Afghan civil war in response to the 11 September 2001 terrorist attacks).

**East Timor**

Between 1999 and 2003 the armed forces of Australia and New Zealand deployed together in a large scale operation in East Timor, to prevent pro-Indonesian militia from overturning a vote for independence and conducting ethnic cleansing on the island. The United States provided only limited logistical support but USS Mobile Bay provided air defence for the initial entry operation. The operation was taken over by the United Nations.

**Taiwan**

One topic that became prominent in the early 2000s are its implications in the case of a hypothetical attack by the People's Republic of China against the Republic of China on Taiwan, who would likely receive American support. While Australia has strong cultural and economic ties with the United States, it also has an increasingly important trade relationship with mainland China.

In August 2004, Foreign Minister Alexander Downer implied in Beijing that the treaty would likely not apply to that situation, but he was quickly corrected by then Prime Minister John Howard. In March 2005, after an official of the People's Republic of China stated that it may be necessary for Australia to reassess the treaty and after the PRC passed an Anti-Secession Law regarding the ROC, Downer stated that in case of a PRC attack on the ROC, the treaty would come into force, but that the treaty would require only consultations with the United States and not necessarily commit Australia to war.

**Current Scenario**

Annual bilateral meetings between the US Secretary of State and the Australian Foreign Minister replaced annual meetings of the ANZUS Council of Foreign Ministers. The first bilateral meeting was held in Canberra in 1985. At the second meeting, in San Francisco in 1986, the United States announced that it was suspending its treaty security obligations to New Zealand pending the restoration of port access. Subsequent bilateral Australia–US Ministerial (AUSMIN) meetings have alternated between Australia and the United States.

The alliance engenders some political controversy in Australia. Particularly after Australian involvement in the 2003 Iraq war, some quarters of Australian society have called for a re-evaluation of the relationship between the two nations. Nonetheless the alliance enjoyed broad support during the Cold War and continues to enjoy broad support in Australia. One commentator in Australia has argued that the treaty should be re-negotiated in the context of terrorism, the modern role of the United Nations and as a purely US–Australian alliance. Australia is also a contributor to the National Missile Defense system.

In May 2006, US Assistant Secretary of State for East Asia and Pacific Affairs, Christopher Hill, described the New Zealand anti-nuclear issue as "a relic", and signalled that the US wanted a closer defence relationship with New Zealand. He also praised New Zealand's involvement in Afghanistan and reconstruction in Iraq. "Rather than trying to change each other's minds on the nuclear issue, which is a bit of a relic, I think we should focus on things we can make work" he told an Australian newspaper.

While there have been signs of the nuclear dispute between the US and NZ thawing out, pressure from the United States increased in 2006 with US trade officials linking the repeal of the ban of American nuclear ships from New Zealand's ports to a potential free trade agreement between the two countries.

On 4 February 2008, US Trade Representative Susan Schwab announced that the United States will join negotiations with four Asia–Pacific countries: Brunei, Chile, New Zealand and Singapore to be known as the "P-4". These nations already have an FTA called the Trans-Pacific Strategic Economic Partnership and the United States will be looking to become involved in the "vitally important emerging Asia-Pacific region" A number of US organisations support the negotiations including, but not limited to: the United States Chamber of Commerce, National Association of Manufacturers, National Foreign Trade Council, Emergency Committee for American Trade and Coalition of Service Industries.

[*Source:* Wikipedia].

## *APPENDIX 4*

## SOUTHEAST ASIA TREATY ORGANIZATION (SEATO)

The Southeast Asia Treaty Organisation (SEATO) was an international organisation for collective defense which was signed on September 8, 1954. The formal institution of SEATO was established at a meeting of treaty partners in Bangkok in February 1955. It was primarily created to block further communist gains in Southeast Asia. The organization's headquarters were located in Bangkok, Thailand. SEATO was dissolved on June 30, 1977. SEATO was planned to be a Southeast Asian version of the North Atlantic Treaty Organization (NATO), in which the military forces of each member would be coordinated to provide for the collective defense of the members' country. SEATO did use portions of the military forces of its members in annual joint training maneuvers. The membership of SEATO reflected a mid-1950s' combination of "out of area" powers and "in area" pro-Western nations. France, the United Kingdom, and the United States represented the strongest Western powers. Australia, Thailand, the Philippines, and New Zealand represented Europeanized or pro-Western nations in the Southeast Asian area.

Pakistan was included not only because East Pakistan (now Bangladesh) was geographically close to Southeast Asia, but possibly because Pakistan was a member of the pro-Western Central Treaty Organization (CENTO) alliance. Thus the pro-Western, anti-communist military alliances of the Mid-east and Southeast Asia were linked by the membership of Pakistan in both. Despite being intended to provide a collective, anti-communist shield to Southeast Asia, SEATO was unable to intervene in the conflicts in Cambodia, Laos, and Vietnam because an intervention required a decision of unanimity, which was never reached; France and the Philippines objected. Intervention in the Vietnam conflict was sought again later, but France and

Pakistan withheld support. Unlike the NATO alliance, SEATO had no joint commands with standing forces. Also unlike NATO, an attack on one member was not automatically considered an attack on all. Consequently, each member could effectively block any or all collective SEATO action. Given the declining interest of France (after 1954) and the United Kingdom (after the end of the Indonesian-Malaysian conflict, in 1966) in Southeast Asia, SEATO failed to be effective as a collective security organization.

Because of the 1954 Accords settling the First Indochina War, South Vietnam, Cambodia, and Laos were not SEATO members. The United States sought, but failed, to make the Vietnam War into a SEATO collective defense problem. Consequently, questions of dissolving the organization arose as early as 1973. Pakistan withdrew on November 7, 1973. and France withdrew on June 30, 1974. The organization formally ended in 1977. Organizationally, SEATO was headed by the Secretary-General, with a council of representatives from member nations and an international staff. In addition to joint military training, the organization did some work on mutual social and economic issues.

SEATO was created as part of the Truman Doctrine of creating anti-communist bilateral and collective defense treaties. These treaties and agreements were intended to create alliances that would contain communist power. This policy was considered to have been largely developed by American diplomat and Soviet expert George F. Kennan. President Dwight D. Eisenhower's Secretary of State John Foster Dulles (1953-1959) was the primary force behind the creation of SEATO, which expanded the concept of anti-communist collective defense to Southeast Asia.

[Source: Wikipedia].

# Bibliography


Ambatkar, Sanjay, 2002. *India and ASEAN in the 21 century*. New Delhi, Anmol.

Abdullah, Taufik, and Sharon Siddique, eds. 1986. *Islam and Society in Southeast Asia*. Singapore: Institute of Southeast Asian Studies.

Ackerman, Susan E., and Raymond L. M. Lee. 1988. "Theory, National Policy and the Management of Minority Cultures," *Southeast Asian Journal of Social Science*, 16.2:132-42.

Adas, Michael. 1979. *Prophets of Rebellion: Millenarian Protest Movements against the European Colonial Order*. Chapel Hill: The University of North Carolina Press.

Adas, Michael. 1988. "Market Demand Versus Imperial Control: Colonial Contradictions and the Origins of Agrarian Conflict in South and Southeast Asia," in *Global Crises and Social Movements: Artisans, Peasants, Populists, and the World Economy*. Edmund Burke, III, ed. Boulder, Colorado: Westview Press.

Adas, Michael. 1992. "From Avoidance to Confrontation: Peasant Protest in Precolonial and Colonial Southeast Asia," in Colonialism and Culture. Nicholas B. Dirks, ed. Ann Arbor: University of Michigan Press. The Comparative Study in Society and History Book Series. Pp. XX-XX.

Adrianoff, David. [1976?]. "The Effect of the Laotian Conflict of Meo Ethnic Identity," in *Intergroup Relations: Asian Scene*. Tai S. Kang, ed. Buffalo, N. Y.: Council on International Studies, State University of New York at Buffalo. Pp. 75-78.

Agrawal, D.P. 1984. "Origin of Metallurgy in Asia: Myth and Reality," In Southeast Asian Archaeology at the XV Pacific Science Congress. Dunedin, New Zealand: University of Otago, University of Otago Studies in Prehistoric Anthropology, Volume 16. Ed. by Donn Bayard. Pp. 161-69.

Ahmat, Sharom, and Sharon Siddique, eds. 1987. *Muslim Society, Higher Education and Development in Southeast Asai*. Singapore: Institute of Southeast Asian Studies.

Barnes, R.H., Andrew Gray, and Benedict Kingsbury, eds. 1995. *Indigenous Peoples of Asia*. Ann Arbor: Association for Asian Studies, Monograph and Occasional Paper Seris, No. 48.

Bayard, Donn. 1983. "The Development of Metallurgy in Southeast Asia: A Reply to Loofs-Wissowa," *Journal of Southeast Asian Studies,* 14.1:12-17.

Bayard, Donn. 1984. "Agriculture, Mettalurgy, and State Formation in Mainland Southeast Asia," *Current Anthropology*, 25.1:103-106.

Bray, Fracesca. 1983. "Patterns of Evolution in Rice-Growing Societies," *Journal of Peasant Studies*, 11:3-33.

·Carroll, Theodora Foster. 1983. *Women, Religion and Development in the Third World*. New York: Praeger.

Catlin, Amy and Dixie Swift. 1987. Textiles as Texts: Arts of Hmong Women from Laos. Los Angeles: The Woman's Building.

Davidson, Jeremy H. C. S., and H. Cordell, eds. 1982. *The Short Story in South East Asia: Aspects of a Genre*. London: School of Oriental and African Studies.

Elek, Andrew. 1991. "Asia Pacific Economic Co-operation," in *Southeast Asia Affairs 1991*. Singapore: Institute of Southeast Asian Studies. Pp. 33-48.

Ellen, Roy F. 1976. "Comment on 'An Evolutionary Approach to the Southeast Asian Cultural Sequence," *Current Anthropology,* 17.2:231.

Ellen, R. F. 1983. "Social Theory, Ethnography and the Understanding of Practical Islam in Southeast Asia," in M. B. Hooker ed., *Islam in Southeast Asia*. Leiden: Brill. Pp.

Elson, Diane, and Ruth Pearson. 1981. "Nimble Fingers Make Cheap Workers: An Analysis of Women's Employment in Third World Export Manufacturing," *Feminist Review*, 7:87-107.

Elson, Robert E. 1992. "International Commerce, the State and Society: Economic and Social Change," *The Cambridge History of Southeast Asia*. Volume Two, The Nineteenth and Twentieth Centuries. Nicholas Tarling, ed. Cambridge: Cambridge University Press.

Feingold, David A., and Jennifer Shanks. 1979. "The Political Ecology of Opium in Highland Southeast Asia," in *IROS: The International Review of Opium Studies*. Philadelphia: ISHI, pp. XXX-XXX.

Fickle, Dorothy H. 1974. "Crowned Buddha Images in Southeast Asia," in *Art and Archeology in Thailand*. Bangkok: Fine Arts Department.

Glover, Ian, et al., eds. 1992. Early Metallurgy, Trade and Urban Centers in Thailand and Southeast Asia. Bangkok: White Lotus.

Gokhale, Balakrishna G., ed. 1966. *Asian Studies One: A Collection of Papers on Aspects of Asian History and Civilization*. Bombay: Popular Prakashan.

Golay, Frank H. 1976. "Southeast Asia: The 'Colonial Drain' Revisited," in *Southeast Asian History and Historiography: Essays Presented to D.G.E. Hall,* ed. by C.D. Cowan and O.W. Wolters. Ithaca, New York: Cornell University Press. Pp. 368-87.

Groslier, Benard Philipe. 1960. "Our Knowledge of Khmer Civiliation: A Re-Appraisal," *Journal of the Siam Society,* 48.1:1-28.

Han, Sang-bok, ed. 1986. *Asian Peoples and Their Cultures: Continuity and Change*. Seoul: Seoul National University Press.

Hart, Gillian. 1989. "Agrarian Change in the Context of State Patronage," in *Agrarian Transformations: Local Processes and the State in Southeast Asia*. Gillian Hart, Andrew Turton, and Benjamin White, eds. Berkeley and Los Angeles: University of California Press.

Hayden, Brian. 1976. "Comment on 'An Evolutionary Approach to the Southeast Asian Cultural Sequence," *Current Anthropology,* 17.2:232-33.

Hirschman, Charles. 1994. "Population and Society in Twentieth-Century Southeast Asia," *Journal of Southeast Asian Studies*, 25.2:381-416.

Hirschman, Charles, Charles F. Keyes, and Karl Hutterer, eds. 1992. *Southeast Asian Studies in the Balance: Reflections from America.* Ann Arbor: Association for Asian Studies.

Hitchcock, M.J., V.T. King, and M.J.G. Parnell, eds. 1992. *Tourism in South-East Asia.* London and New York: Routledge.

Iyer, Pico. 1988. *Video Night in Kathmandu and Other Reports from the Not-So-Far East.* New York: Alfred A. Knopf. (New York: Viking, 1989).

Jones, Gavin W. 1988. "Urbanization Trends in Southeast Asia: Some Issues for Policy," *Journal of Southeast Asian Studies,* 19.1:137-54.

Karim Wazir Jahan. 1995. "Bilateralism and Gender in Southeast Asia," *'Male' and 'Female' in Developing Southeast Asia.* Wazir Jahan Karim, ed. Oxford and Washington, D.C.: Berg Publishers.

Kathirithamby-Wells, J. 1992. "The Age of Transition: The Mid-Eighteenth to the Early Nineteenth Century," *The Cambridge History of Southeast Asia.* Volume One,

From Early Times to c. 1800. Nicholas Tarling, ed. Cambridge: Cambridge University Press.

Kingsbury, Benedict. 1995. "'Indigenous Peoples' as an International Legal Concept," in *Indigenous Peoples of Asia*. R.H. Barnes, Andrew Gray, and Benedict Kingsbury, eds. Ann Arbor: Association for Asian Studies, Monograph and Occasional Paper Seris, No. 48. Pp. 13-34.

Krause, Gerald H., ed. 1988. *Urban Society in Southeast Asia*. Volume II: Poltical and Cultural Issues. Hong Kong: Asian Research Service, Asian Studies Monograph Series.

Lieberman, Victor. 1995. "An Age of Commerce in Southeast Asia? Problems of Regional Coherence — A Review Article," *Journal of Asian Studies*, 54.3:796-815.

Mackie, Jamie. 1992. "Changing Patterns in Big Business in Southeast Asia," *Southeast Asian Capitalists*. Ruth McVey, ed. Ithaca, N.Y.: Cornell University Southeast Asian Studies.

Manderson, Lenore, ed. 1986. *Shared Wealth and Symbol: Food, Culture and Society in Oceania and Southeast Asia*. Cambridge: Cambridge University Press.

Muzaffar, Chandra. 1986. "Islamic Resurgence: A Global View," in *Islam and Society in Southeast Asia*. Taufik Abdullah and Sharon Siddique, eds. Singapore: Institute of Southeast Asian Studies.

Parnwell, Michael, and Raymond Bryant, eds. 1996. *Environmental Change in South-East Asia*. New York: Routledge.

Postlethwaite, T. Neville, and R. Murray Thomas, eds. 1980. *Schooling in the ASEAN Region: Primary and Secondary Education in Indonesia, Malaysia, the Philippines, Singapore, and Thailand*. New York: Pergamon Press.

Pudaita, L.A. 2009. *Mizoram and Look East Policy*. New Delhi: Akansha.

Sandhu, Kernial Singh. 1981. "Southeast Asian Studies: Some Unresolved Problems," *A Colloquium on Southeast Asian Studies*. Tunku Shamsul Bahrin, Chandran Jeshurun, and A. Terry Rambo, eds. Singapore: Institute of Southeast Asian Studies.

Sardesai, D.R. 1989. *Southeast Asia: Past and Present*. 2nd edition. Boulder: Westview Press.

Shiratori, Yoshiro. 1957. "A Question of the Ancient History of Thai," *Abstracts* of Paper [presented at the 9th Pacific Science Congress, Bangkok, 1957), pp. 22-23.

Sinha, P.C. 1997. *50 Years of United Nations and World Affairs,* New Delhi, Anmol.

Sinha, P.C. 2006. *Encyclopaedia of Southeast and Far East Asia,* New Delhi, Anmol.

Somsak Phansomboon. 1957. "A Bioseriological Consideration of the Migration of the Thai Race: A Preliminary Report of a New Concept," *Journal of the Siam Society*, 45.2:55-63.

Suryadinata, Leo, ed. 1997. *Ethnic Chinese as Southeast Asians*. Singapore: Institute of Southeasts Asian Studies.

Taylor, R.H. 1993. "Political Science and South East Asian Studies," *South East Asia Research*, 1.1:5-26.

Taylor, R.H., ed. 1996. *The Politics of Elections in Southeast Asia*. Washington, D.C.: Woodrow Wilson Center Press and Cambridge: Cambridge University Press.

Turley, William S., ed. 1985. *Confrontation or Coexistence: The Future of ASEAN-Vietnam Relations*. Bangkok: Chulalongkorn University, Institute of Secruity and International Studies.

Vatikiotis, Michael R.J. 1996. Political Change in Southeast Asia. London and New York: Routledge.

Yong Mun Cheong. 1992. "The Political Structures of the

Independent States," *The Cambridge History of Southeast Asia*. Volume Two, The Nineteenth and Twentieth Centuries. Nicholas Tarling, ed. Cambridge: Cambridge University Press. Pp. 387-466.

Yousof, Ghulam-Sarwar. 1994. *Dictionary of Traditional South-East Asian Theatre*. Singapore: Oxford University Press for the Institute of Southeast Asian Studies.

# Index

## S



## T



## U



## V



## W



## Z